CHARMED KNITS

PROJECTS
FOR FANS OF
HARRY POTTER®

Alison Hansel

BICENTENNIAL
1807
WILEY
2007
BICENTENNIAL

Wiley Publishing, Inc.

For general information on our other products and services or to obtain technical support please contact our Customer Care Department within the U.S. at (800) 762-2974, outside the U.S. at (317) 572-3993 or fax (317) 572-4002.

Wiley also publishes its books in a variety of electronic formats. Some content that appears in print may not be available in electronic books. For more information about Wiley products, please visit our web site at www.wiley.com.

Library of Congress Cataloging-in-Publication Data:
Hansel, Alison.
Charmed knits : projects for fans of Harry Potter / Alison Hansel.
    p. cm.
Includes bibliographical references and index.
ISBN-13: 978-0-470-06731-4 (pbk. : alk. paper)
ISBN-10: 0-470-06731-4 (alk. paper)
1. Knitting—Patterns. 2. Rowling, J. K.—Characters—Harry Potter. I. Title.
TT820.H263 2007
746.43'2041—dc22

                          2007003154

Printed in the United States of America

10 9 8 7 6 5 4 3 2 1

Book production by Wiley Publishing, Inc., Composition Services

Wiley Bicentennial Logo: Richard J. Pacifico

CREDITS

Acquisitions Editor
Roxane Cerda

Project Editor
Kitty Wilson Jarrett

Technical Editors
Jean Lampe, Alison Guinee, Amy O'Neill Houck,
Sharon Turner, Amy Swenson, Alexandra Virgiel

Editorial Manager
Christina Stambaugh

Publisher
Cindy Kitchel

Vice President and Executive Publisher
Kathy Nebenhaus

Interior Design
Melissa Auciello-Brogan

Cover Design
José Almaguer

Photography
Matt Bowen

Photographic Assistant
Andrew Hanson

Special Thanks . . .

To the following companies for providing the yarn for the projects shown in this book:

- ☾ Cascade Yarns
- ☾ Classic Elite Yarns
- ☾ HipKnits
- ☾ JCA/Jo Sharp
- ☾ Knit Picks
- ☾ Lion Brand Yarn
- ☾ Misti International
- ☾ Plymouth Yarn
- ☾ Tilli Thomas Specialty Yarns
- ☾ Westminster Fibers/Rowan and Jaeger Yarns

*To all the children who inspire us to write and
knit and believe. They are truly magical.*

ACKNOWLEDGMENTS

This book would not have been possible without the help of many wizards. First and foremost, thank you to all the designers for sharing their magic spells and to all the editors who understand the mysterious ways that books get made. Special thanks to Jean, the technical editor, for doing a miraculous job standardizing patterns from such a wide and varied range of designers and to the other reviewers who jumped in at the end with their circled spectacles to lend us another pair of eyes. Thanks also to my wonderful knitting buddies Johanna, Colleen, and Lisa, who eagerly whipped out their magic needles to help knit samples.

A Hagrid-sized thank you is owed to my husband and two boys, who not only put up with yarns, projects, and boxes spilling out of the cupboard under the stairs for six months but also my repeatedly disapparating while finishing the book.

Final thanks go to the entire online knitting community, which has fueled the huge knitting phenomenon of recent years and helped create a full and fantastic world of Harry Potter knitting. And, of course, to J.K. Rowling for inspiring us all with her wonderful vision of a world where knitting needles can work magic.

ABOUT THE AUTHOR

Alison Hansel is a popular knitting blogger whose daily knitting-related missives can be read on the blue blog at alison. knitsmiths.us. She started knitting in 2001 while on bed rest with her twins and started blogging about it in 2002, when those twins let her start knitting again. She became an avid Harry Potter fan after seeing those Weasley twins and those Weasley sweaters in the first movie and has since designed several Potter-inspired patterns as well as hosted several highly popular Weasley knit-alongs on her blog. She occasionally knits other things (like socks for her Sockapalooza sock exchanges) but always finds herself drawn back to scarlet and gold before long. She has published patterns in the popular online knitting magazines MagKnits and Knitty.com and in the recently published *Big Girl Knits* and forthcoming *Handpainted Yarns*.

Alison lives in Boston, with her husband, who thankfully is as patient and understanding as Richard Harris's Dumbledore, her twin boys, who have no idea what the H on their sweaters really stands for, and a baby girl on the way, whom her husband will very sensibly not let her name Fred.

TABLE OF CONTENTS

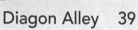
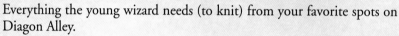

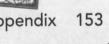
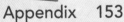

INTRODUCTION

It may at first seem surprising that the magical world J.K. Rowling creates in the Harry Potter series is filled with knitting. In each book, we catch another glimpse of one of her characters taking up the needles: Hagrid knits something huge and yellow while escorting Harry to Diagon Alley for the first time; Mrs. Weasley charms up sweaters for her entire clan every year; Hermione learns to knit in an attempt to free the Gryffindor house-elves with hats and scarves; Dobby saves his money to buy yarn and knit Christmas socks for Harry; and even Dumbledore admits that he enjoys reading a good knitting pattern! Gradually, one begins to sense that the rather humble craft of knitting is somehow at home in this fantastical world full of magical mirrors and maps, flying brooms and floo powder, and mind-boggling time-turners and portkeys.

But why should we be surprised to find that there just might be a genuine connection between the traditional art of knitting and the ancient art of magic? Isn't knitting itself a form of alchemy: giving form to fiber, shaping yarn into useful objects, conjuring a sweater from a sheep's wool? A knitting pattern, much like a magic spell, is a set of instructions for transfiguration, a set of phrases and commands that appear mysterious to uninitiated Muggles but to students of the art reveal a process of metamorphosis as magical as any in the wizarding world.

Perhaps this is why Rowling's rich world, with its combination of the traditional and the fantastic, has been such an inspiration to so many knitters. The books and films have inspired people to learn to knit so they can make their own genuine house scarves or sweaters. And they've also inspired knitters to start designing. From sweaters to cellphone cozies, knitters have designed dozens of unique, imaginative items drawn from what they've read in the books or seen in the movies. This book has grown from that spirit and brings together some of the best of those now almost cult patterns, along with a host of new ones.

There are designers here whose names you will recognize from knitting publications or the Internet, and there are also many fans-turned-designer whose names may be new to you. But because they are all fans, you can be sure that their patterns reflect a love for the characters and a respect for the marvelous world Rowling has created. They just may transport you into that magical world through knitting.

A Journey of Stitchcraft and Wizardry

This book takes us on a knitting journey through the world of Harry Potter. It begins where Harry begins every year—with a visit to the Burrow. Who else could usher us into this new world of stitchcraft but the mother knitter herself, Mrs. Weasley? In the "Weasley Knits" section, we get a first look at the wonders this world has to offer, and, in true Weasley style, the patterns range from functional to funky to full-on fantastic. Up next is a trip to Diagon Alley to get new wizard knitters supplied with all the necessities of the wizard world. You can't start working your magic without a wizard hat and wand cozy for those magic needles! At last we arrive at Hogwarts and are sorted into houses. The "House Colors" section, at the heart of the book, offers a myriad of patterns all sporting the signature house stripes seen in the films. Scarves, hats, socks—you can knit yourself an entire uniform! With the arrival of the holidays, the "Magic of Giving" takes over. Giving handknits to others is a natural part of the tradition of knitting, and wizard knitters are no different from Muggle knitters in this case—they just sometimes make more interesting things. The final section of the book, "Home at Hogwarts," is for those knitters who, like Harry, feel more at home in the wizarding world of Hogwarts than in the Muggle world of Privet Drive. Who wants to go back to knitting the same old Muggle wear when even the most casual wizard garb is so appealing?

Although the patterns in this book were inspired by items mentioned in the books or seen in the films, they aren't limited to being merely Harry Potter tribute items. All the patterns would make fun, practical items for anyone to wear and use anytime. Who wouldn't love a comfy, oversized initial sweater like the Weasley sweater? What knitter doesn't dream of a great knitting bag like Mrs. Weasley's or Hermione's? A sporty ribbed jersey like the Quidditch Sweater or classically cabled sweater like Harry's Red Cable Sweater would be perfect for any young lad. Change up the colors in the "House Colors" garments, and you've got wonderful basic patterns for all your winter wear.

Charming Your Needles: How to Use This Book

Each pattern includes a stitch guide that details the stitch patterns as well as a list of any special techniques used in that pattern. And each has a difficulty rating that every student of Hogwarts will recognize:

- ☾ *First Year* patterns are perfect for beginning wizards who know how to charm up knits and purls and are ready to try out a new spell or two.

- ☾ Patterns rated at the *Ordinary Wizarding Level (O.W.L.)* are for intermediate wizard knitters comfortable with all the basic knitting charms, including shaping techniques (increasing and decreasing) and general seaming methods.

- ☾ The *Nastily Exhausting Wizarding Test (N.E.W.T.)* patterns are for the most experienced wizard knitters. No surprise we find these patterns in Mrs. Weasley's home!

There's also a standard book of spells in the back of the book to help you find your way through the abbreviations and techniques you might not be familiar with.

I hope you enjoy this book and its patterns as much as I enjoyed dreaming it up. It was a pleasure to live in this world for a while—a world where the magical qualities of knitting are recognized and appreciated and where all knitters can become wizards.

Weasley Knits

When the Weasley welcome wagon comes wheeling over to Harry at the entrance to Platform 9¾, we know he's in for a wonderful journey. The Weasleys are Harry's introduction to the magical world, and Mrs. Weasley, as an avid knitter, serves as our introduction to the world of Harry Potter knitting. She is an inspiration for knitters, both magical and Muggle. From her holiday jumpers to her own colorful knitwear, she teaches us that while wizards may not need telephones or cars, they can always use a handknit sweater.

   These patterns take us on a trip to the Burrow, where we find not only the now-classic Weasley sweater and Molly's outrageous ruffled housecoat, but also her special bag of stitch witchery and the incredible clock she uses to keep track of her brood. And the Burrow wouldn't be complete without the Weasleys' shabby old owl, Errol! These uncommon, funky knits capture the style of the entire Weasley family and show that wizard knitting can be as strange and as marvelous as you can imagine.

Materials

- Jo Sharp *Silkroad Aran Tweed* (85% wool, 10% silk, 5% cashmere, 104 yd. [95 m] per 50 g ball), #129 Enamel (color A), 4 (6, 9, 11, 13, 15, 17, 20) balls, and #114 Vermouth (color B), 1 ball

- Or similar yarn that knits to specified gauge: heavy-worsted-weight wool or wool-blend yarn, about 400 (595, 855, 1,090, 1,310, 1,510, 1,760, 2,010) yd. [366 (544, 782, 997, 1,198, 1,381, 1,609, 1,838) m]

- US 8 [5 mm] needles

- US 8 [5 mm] 16" [40 cm] circular needle

- Stitch holder

- Stitch markers

- Tapestry needle

Gauge

16 sts and 24 rows = 4" [10 cm] in St st using size 8 [5 mm] needles

THE WEASLEY SWEATER

Designer – Alison Hansel ☾ *Pattern Rating – First Year*

Weasley sweaters for everyone! Just like the sweaters Mrs. Weasley made for her kids and Harry for Christmas in the first movie, this simple oversized sweater is knit in a tweedy yarn with an initial on the front. The sweater is a basic, drop-shoulder style, with sleeves knit down from the body of the sweater so there's minimal seaming. And because it's knit at such a comfortable gauge and is oversized, this project is great for a beginner charming up a sweater for the first time. The initial can even be worked into the front with duplicate stitch! The soft and rather luxurious tweedy cashmere blend balances the intentional homeliness of the sweater: It may have the look of Weasley clothes, but it feels divine! And don't worry about it being perfect—Molly wouldn't.

Back

With color A, CO 50 (58, 66, 74, 82, 90, 98, 106) sts.

Work in St st, as described in the stitch guide, until piece measures 13 (16, 20, 24, 26, 28, 30, 32)" [33 (40.5, 51, 61, 66, 71, 76, 81.5) cm] from CO edge (uncurl lower edge to measure correctly), ending with a WS row completed.

Shape Shoulders

Next row (RS): BO 15 (17, 20, 22, 25, 27, 30, 32) sts, knit to end.

Next row (WS): BO 15 (17, 20, 22, 25, 27, 30, 32) sts, purl to end.

Place rem 20 (24, 26, 30, 32, 36, 38, 42) sts on st holder for the neck.

Mark beg of armhole by measuring 6 (7½, 9, 10, 11, 12, 13, 14)" [15 (19, 23, 25.5, 28, 30.5, 33, 35.5) cm] down from each shoulder and tying scraps of yarn through the edge st at each end of row to use as markers.

Front

Work as for back until piece measures 4½ (6½, 9½, 12½, 13½, 15½, 16½, 18½)" [11.5 (16.5, 24, 31.5, 34.5, 39, 42, 47) cm] from CO edge (uncurl lower edge to measure correctly), ending with a WS row completed.

At this point, you need to decide whether to add the H now, using the intarsia method, or continue knitting in color A and add the H later, using duplicate stitch.

Adding H with Duplicate Stitch Only

If you plan to add the initial H later by using duplicate stitch, continue knitting in St st until piece measures 10½ (13, 17½, 20½, 22, 24, 25½, 27½)" [26.5 (33, 44.5, 52, 56, 61, 65, 70) cm] from CO edge (uncurl edge to measure correctly), ending with a WS row completed.

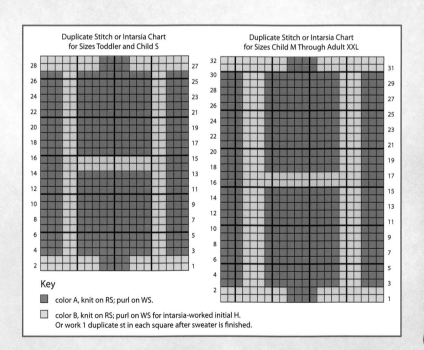

Duplicate Stitch or Intarsia Chart for Sizes Toddler and Child S

Duplicate Stitch or Intarsia Chart for Sizes Child M Through Adult XXL

Key

■ color A, knit on RS; purl on WS.

□ color B, knit on RS; purl on WS for intarsia-worked initial H.
Or work 1 duplicate st in each square after sweater is finished.

Finished Size

Toddler (Child S, Child M, Child L/Adult S, Adult M, Adult L, Adult XL, Adult XXL)

To fit chest: 20 (24, 28, 32, 36, 40, 44, 48)" [51 (61, 71, 81.5, 91.5, 101.5, 112, 122) cm]

Circumference: 24 (28, 32, 36, 40, 44, 48, 52)" [61 (71, 81.5, 91.5, 101.5, 112, 122, 132) cm]

Length: 13 (16, 20, 24, 26, 28, 30, 32)" [33 (40.5, 51, 61, 66, 71, 76, 81.5) cm]

Sample shown: Size Child M

Note: This sweater includes a lot of ease because it looks so great oversized!

Stitch Guide for This Project

Stockinette Stitch (St st) Worked in Rows

Row 1 (RS): Knit.

Row 2 (WS): Purl.

Rep rows 1 and 2.

Double Rib (2x2) Worked in Rows over a Multiple of 4 Sts Plus 2

Row 1: *K2, p2; rep from * to last 2 sts, k2.

Row 2: P2, *k2, p2; rep from * to end of row.

Rep rows 1 and 2.

Stockinette Stitch (St st) Worked in Rounds

Knit all sts.

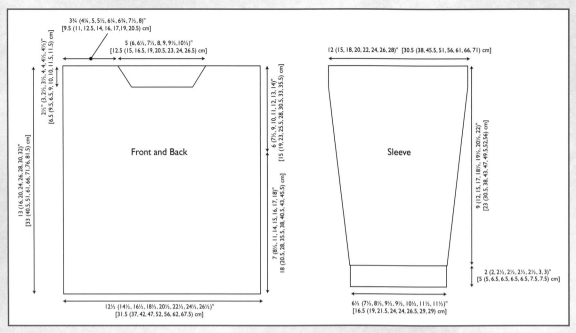

Front and Back

3¾ (4¼, 5, 5½, 6¼, 6¾, 7½, 8)"
[9.5 (11, 12.5, 14, 16, 17, 19, 20.5) cm]

5 (6, 6½, 7½, 8, 9, 9½, 10½)"
[12.5 (15, 16.5, 19, 20.5, 23, 24, 26.5) cm]

2½" (3, 3½, 3½, 4, 4, 4½, 4½)"
[6.5 (9.5, 6.5, 9, 10, 10, 11.5, 11.5) cm]

13 (16, 20, 24, 26, 28, 30, 32)"
[33 (40.5, 51, 61, 66, 71, 76, 81.5) cm]

6 (7½, 9, 10, 11, 12, 13, 14)"
[15 (19, 23, 25.5, 28, 30.5, 33, 35.5) cm]

7 (8½, 11, 14, 15, 16, 17, 18)"
[18 (20.5, 28, 35.5, 38, 40.5, 43, 45.5) cm]

12½ (14½, 16½, 18½, 20½, 22½, 24½, 26½)"
[31.5 (37, 42, 47, 52, 56, 62, 67.5) cm]

Sleeve

12 (15, 18, 20, 22, 24, 26, 28)" [30.5 (38, 45.5, 51, 56, 61, 66, 71) cm]

9 (12, 15, 17, 18½, 19½, 20½, 22)"
[23 (30.5, 38, 43, 47, 49.5, 52, 56) cm]

2 (2, 2½, 2½, 2½, 2½, 3, 3)"
[5 (5, 6.5, 6.5, 6.5, 6.5, 7.5, 7.5) cm]

6½ (7½, 8½, 9½, 9½, 10½, 11½, 11½)"
[16.5 (19, 21.5, 24, 24, 26.5, 29, 29) cm]

Adding H with Intarsia Method Only

To knit the initial H using the intarsia method, center the H as follows:

Row 1 (RS): K15 (19, 22, 26, 30, 34, 38, 42) sts in color A, then follow row 1 in the appropriate color chart (see page 3) for the size you're making, joining new ball of yarn for each separate color and twisting the yarns around each other when switching colors to avoid gaps in the work.

Continue following chart over the center 20 (20, 22, 22, 22, 22, 22, 22) charted sts. When chart row 1 is complete, join new ball of color A and knit rem 15 (19, 22, 26, 30, 34, 38, 42) sts.

When the charted rows are finished, continue working in St st with color A only until piece measures 10½ (13, 17½, 20½, 22, 24, 25½, 27½)" [26.5 (33, 44.5, 52, 56, 61, 65, 70) cm] from CO edge (uncurl edge to measure correctly), ending with a WS row completed.

Shape Neck Opening

Next row (RS): K31 (36, 40, 45, 49, 54, 59, 64), slip last 12 (14, 14, 16, 16, 18, 20, 22) sts worked onto stitch holder for center neck, k19 (22, 26, 29, 33, 36, 39, 42).

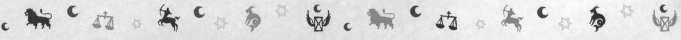

Work right shoulder (as worn) sts only:

Row 1 (WS): Purl to last 3 sts before neck opening, p2tog, p1—18 (21, 25, 28, 32, 35, 38, 41) sts rem.

Row 2 (RS): K1, k2tog, knit to end of row—17 (20, 24, 27, 31, 34, 37, 40) sts rem.

Rep last 2 rows 0 (0, 1, 1, 2, 2, 2, 3) times more—17 (20, 22, 25, 27, 30, 33, 34) sts rem.

Next row (WS): Purl.

Next row (RS): K1, k2tog, knit to end of row— 16 (19, 21, 24, 26, 29, 32, 33) sts rem.

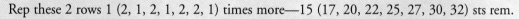

Rep these 2 rows 1 (2, 1, 2, 1, 2, 2, 1) times more—15 (17, 20, 22, 25, 27, 30, 32) sts rem.

Continue in St st without further shaping until piece measures 13 (16, 20, 24, 26, 28, 30, 32)" [33 (40.5, 51, 61, 66, 71, 76, 81.5) cm] from CO edge (uncurl edge to measure correctly), ending with a RS row completed.

Next row (WS): BO rem 15 (17, 20, 22, 25, 27, 30, 32) sts pwise.

Join yarn at armhole edge of left side (as worn) and shape neck and shoulders as for right side, reversing all shapings, as follows:

Row 1 (RS): Knit to last 3 sts before neck opening, ssk, k1—18 (21, 25, 28, 32, 35, 38, 41) sts rem.

Row 2 (WS): P1, p2tog, purl to end of row—17 (20, 24, 27, 31, 34, 37, 40) sts rem.

Rep these 2 rows 0 (0, 1, 1, 2, 2, 2, 3) times more—17 (20, 22, 25, 27, 30, 33, 34) sts rem.

Next row (RS): Knit.

Next row (WS): P1, p2tog, purl to end of row—16 (19, 21, 24, 26, 29, 32, 33) sts rem.

Rep these 2 rows 1 (2, 1, 2, 1, 2, 2, 1) times more—15 (17, 20, 22, 25, 27, 30, 32) sts rem.

Continue in St st without further shaping until piece measures 13 (16, 20, 24, 26, 28, 30, 32)" [33 (40.5, 51, 61, 66, 71, 76, 81.5) cm] from CO edge (uncurl edge to measure correctly), ending with a WS row completed.

Next row (RS): BO rem 15 (17, 20, 22, 25, 27, 30, 32) sts.

Mark beg of armhole by measuring 6 (7½, 9, 10, 11, 12, 13, 14)" [15 (19, 23, 25.5, 28, 30.5, 33, 35.5) cm] down from each shoulder and tying a spare scrap of yarn around edge st.

Sew shoulder seams together using backstitch (see page 159) or grafting (see page 160).

Sleeves

With RS facing, pick up 48 (60, 72, 80, 88, 96, 104, 112) sts between front and back armhole markers on one side of body.

Beg with WS row, work in St st for 5 (9, 11, 11, 11, 11, 9, 3) rows.

Sleeve Decreases

Dec row (RS): K1, k2tog, knit to last 3 sts, ssk, k1—46 (58, 70, 78, 86, 94, 102, 110) sts.

Rep dec row every 4th row 10 (14, 18, 20, 24, 26, 28, 32) times more—26 (30, 34, 38, 38, 42, 46, 46) sts.

Work even until sleeve measures 9 (12, 15, 17, 18½, 19½, 20½, 22)" [23 (30.5, 38, 43, 47, 49.5, 52, 56) cm], ending with a WS row completed.

Cuff

Row 1 (RS): *K2, p2; rep from * to last 2 sts, k2.

Row 2 (WS): P2, *k2, p2; rep from * to end of row.

Rep rows 1 and 2 until cuff measures 2 (2, 2½, 2½, 2½, 2½, 3, 3)" [5 (5, 6.5, 6.5, 6.5, 6.5, 7.5, 7.5) cm]. BO in patt.

Work second sleeve same as first.

Neck

Return back neck sts to needle, join new yarn at right edge (as worn) of back neck, and, with 16" [40 cm] circular needle, knit across 20 (24, 26, 30, 32, 36, 38, 42) sts from back neck. Pick up and k10 (12, 14, 14, 16, 16, 18, 18) sts along left side of neck. Place 12 (14, 14, 16, 16, 18, 20, 22) front neck sts on needle and knit across sts. Pick up and k10 (12, 14, 14, 16, 16, 18, 18) sts along right side of neck—52 (62, 68, 74, 80, 86, 94, 100) sts.

Pm to note beg of rnd and join in a circle, being careful not to twist sts. Knit every rnd for 2 (2, 2, 2½, 2½, 2½, 3, 3)" [5 (5, 5, 6.5, 6.5, 6.5, 7.5, 7.5) cm]. BO loosely.

Finishing

Block all pieces to size, according to yarn manufacturer's instructions.

If you did not use the intarsia method, add initial with duplicate st (see page 157).

Sew side and sleeve seams using mattress st (see page 160).

Weave in all rem ends.

Other Recommended Colors

For Ron: Jo Sharp *Silkroad Aran Tweed* #127 Posie (color A)

For the Weasley twins: Jo Sharp *Silkroad Aran Tweed* #126 Highland (color A)

For Percy: Jo Sharp *Silkroad Aran Tweed* #141 Bark (color A)

Materials

- Cascade *220* (100% Peruvian Highland Wool; 220 yd. [201 m] per 100 g skein), #8886 Eggplant (color A), 2 skeins, and #8914 Spring Green (color B), 1 skein; Cascade *220 Quatro* (100% Peruvian Highland Wool; 220 yd. [201 m] per 100 g skein), #9433 Raspberry (color C), 2 skeins, and #9436 Coral (color D), 1 skein
- Or similar yarn that knits to specified gauge: worsted-weight wool or wool-blend yarn, about 305 yd. [279 m] of color A, 100 yd. [92 m] of color B, 340 yd. [311 m] of color C, and 115 yd. [105 m] of color D
- US 5 [3.75 mm] 24" [60 cm] circular needle
- US 5 [3.75 mm] 16" [40 cm] circular needle
- US F [3.75 mm] crochet hook
- Stitch markers
- Stitch holders
- Tapestry needle
- 1 set purse handles
- 1 skein DMC embroidery floss to match side panels
- Sewing needle and thread
- 1 yd. [1 m] lining fabric and heavy-weight interfacing (optional)

MRS. WEASLEY'S BAG OF STITCH WITCHERY

Designer – Alison Stewart-Guinee ☾
Pattern Rating – Ordinary Wizarding Level

Here's the bag that Molly reaches for as she heads out of the Burrow. It is big enough to hold everything a witch on the go might need: wand, clock (for keeping track of loved ones), and, of course, knitting. Although the pattern looks complicated, a little stitch witchery makes this piece a joy to knit. The colorwork sections are knit as four separate panels in slipstitch patterns. This means only one strand of yarn is in use at any given time. The panels are joined together with a variation of a three-needle bind-off, and from there, stitches are picked up and knitted in the round to form the base and the top edge of the bag. Voila . . . no seams— it's like magic!

Instructions

Center Front and Back Panels

Note: Make two panels the same—one for the back and one for the front.

CO 45 sts with color C. Purl 1 row. Then work as follows:

Row 1 (RS): With color D, k5, *sl 1 wyib, sl 1 wyif, sl 1 wyib, k5; rep from * to end of row.

Row 2: With color D, k1, p3, k1, *sl 1 wyif, sl 1 wyib, sl 1 wyif, k1, p3, k1; rep from * to end of row.

Row 3: With color A, k1, *sl 1 wyib, sl 1 wyif, sl 1 wyib, k5; rep from * to end of row, ending last rep with k1 instead of k5.

Row 4: With color A, k1, *sl 1 wyif, sl 1 wyib, sl 1 wyif, k1, p3, k1; rep from * to last 4 sts, sl 1 wyif, sl 1 wyib, sl 1 wyif, k1.

Rows 5 and 6: With color C, rep rows 1 and 2.

Rows 7 and 8: With color D, rep rows 3 and 4.

Rows 9 and 10: With color A, rep rows 1 and 2.

Rows 11 and 12: With color C, rep rows 3 and 4.

Rep these 12 rows 9 times more. Do not BO sts; instead, cut yarn, leaving an 8" [20.5cm] tail, and transfer work to a holder.

Note: The sts on the holders will form the foundation round of the facing at the top edge of the bag.

Side Panels

Note: Make two side panels the same.

CO 65 sts with color A. Then work as follows:

Row 1 (RS): With color C, k2, *[k1, yo, k1] in the next st, k3; rep from * to end of row, ending last rep with k2 instead of k3—97 sts.

Row 2: With color A, p2, *sl 3 wyif, p3; rep from * to end of row, ending last rep with p2 instead of p3.

Row 3: With color A, k1, *k2tog, sl 1 wyib, ssk, k1; rep from * to end of row—65 sts.

Row 4: With color C, p4, *sl 1 wyif, p3; rep from * to last st, p1.

Row 5: With color C, k4, *[k1, yo, k1] in the next st, k3; rep from * to last st, k1—95 sts.

Row 6: With color A, p4, *sl 3 wyif, p3; rep from * to last st, p1.

Row 7: With color A, k3, *k2tog, sl 1 wyib, ssk, k1; rep from* to last 2 sts, k2—65 sts.

Row 8: With color C, p2, *sl 1 wyif, p3; rep from * to end of row, ending last rep with p2 instead of p3.

Rep rows 1–8 until the length of this panel matches that of the center panels. Do not BO sts. Cut yarn, leaving an 8" [20.5 cm] tail, and place sts on a holder.

Note: The sts on the holders will form the foundation round of the facing at the top edge of the bag.

Gauge

21 sts and 24 rows = 4" [10 cm] in slip st pattern using size 5 [3.75 mm] needles

Finished Size

Height: 11" [28 cm]

Width: 18½" [45.5 cm]

Base: 6" x 17" [15 cm x 43 cm]

Stitch Guide for This Project

Garter Stitch Worked in Rounds

Rnd 1: Knit.

Rnd 2: Purl.

Rep rnds 1 and 2.

Note: This pattern uses some crochet techniques. For instructions on how to accomplish the basic crochet stitches, please see the appendix "Special Knitting Techniques."

Joining the Panels

Note: When joining the panels together, you pick up sts along two edges, using a crocheted three-needle bind-off that also forms a picot edging. You pick up sts with the RS facing and with the sts on the holders at the same end.

With RS of one of the center panels facing, use circ needle and color B to pick up and k52 sts between CO edge and top edge, ignoring the held sts. Put aside. With the RS of one of the side panel pieces facing, use second circ needle and color B to pick up and k52 sts between top edge and CO edge.

Hold the needles with the picked-up sts on them parallel, tips together, with the WS of the panels facing each other and both sets of held, top-edge sts at the same end. Insert the crochet hook through the first st on each needle as if working a three-needle bind-off (see page 161). Still using color B, wrap the yarn around the tip of the crochet hook from back to front and draw the loop on the hook through both sts, pulling the 2 sts off both knitting needles. Chain 3 sts by wrapping yarn around the crochet hook and pulling a loop through the st on the hook three times.

*Insert the hook through the next st on each of the two knitting needles. Wrap the yarn around the crochet hook and pull the loop on the hook through the sts on the knitting needles as before, slipping the 2 sts off the needles. You should now have 2 sts on the crochet hook. Pull the st farthest from the tip of the hook over the first st and off the hook. Chain 3 sts and rep from * until 1 st rem on each needle. Work these sts as you did the previous sts, omitting the chain 3. Cut yarn, leaving an 8" [20.5cm] tail, pull the tail through the last loop, and fasten off.

Rep this entire process, using color B to pick up sts on RS along the side edges of each front and side panel, and joining them as established with top edges lined up, until the panels are all connected to form a tube, with the live sts running around the top edge. Weave in all tails and loose ends.

Facing

Note: For added strength and body, the top of the bag is finished with a facing.

To complete the facing, put the live sts from the holders on a 24" [60 cm] circular needle. Pm at one of the crocheted seams to indicate beg of rnd—220 sts.

With color A, RS facing, and beg with first st after marker, knit 1 rnd.

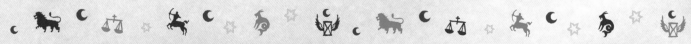

Work turning ridge by purling 1 rnd, then knitting 1 more rnd. Join color D and begin slip st stripe pattern, as follows:

Rnds 1 and 2: With color D, *sl 1 wyib, k1; rep from * to end of rnd.

Rnds 3 and 4: With color A, *k1, sl 1 wyib; rep from * to end of rnd.

Rep these 4 rnds 5 times more.

Then, with color A, knit 1 rnd, purl 1 rnd, and knit 1 rnd. BO sts knitwise.

Bag Base

Note: To make the bottom of the bag, you pick up sts along the bottom edge of the piece and join to work in the round. After making a turning ridge, you work the base in garter st, decreasing at the corners every other round to give the base its rectangular shape. You finish off the base with a three-needle bind-off.

With color C and 24" [60 cm] circular needle, pick up 220 sts along the bottom edge of the bag, as follows: Hold the bag right-side out and upside-down, with a center panel facing you. Begin picking up at the crocheted seam to the left of the center panel. Pick up and k20 sts, pm, pick up and k26 sts, pm, pick up and k84 sts, pm, pick up and k26 sts, pm, pick up and k64 sts, then place a final marker in a contrasting color—220 sts. This last marker signifies the beginning of the rnd, and the four others indicate where shaping occurs.

Work turning ridge: Still using C, purl 2 rnds.

With color B, knit 1 rnd and then purl 1 rnd.

Shape base as follows:

Rnd 1: With color C, *knit to within 2 sts of marker, ssk, slip marker, k2tog; rep from * 3 times more, knit to end of rnd—8 sts decreased.

Rnd 2: With color C, purl.

Rnd 3: With color A, rep rnd 1.

Rnd 4: With color A, purl.

Rnds 5–28: Rep last 4 rnds 5 times more—124 sts.

Rnd 29: With color C, knit. Cut yarn, leaving an 8" [20.5cm] tail.

Divide sts onto two needles so that you have 62 sts on each needle—60 sts from each center section and 1 st from each side panel. With color C and with RS facing, and starting at the end closest to the beg of the rnd, work a three-needle bind-off (see page 161).

Note: While seams are usually worked on the inside of the work, the little ridge formed by binding off on the outside of the piece mimics the garter st pattern nicely and is preferable in this case.

Finishing

Weave in all rem loose ends.

Unlined Bag

Fold facing over at the turning ridge and whipstitch (see page 160) sew into place.

Note: If omitting the lining, consider sewing ribbon or bias tape into the facing of your bag for added strength and to ensure that the weight of the handles doesn't stretch out your knitting.

Lined Bag (Optional)

The sample bag shown here is lined with quilted fabric and heavy-weight interfacing. This gives the bag added stability and helps the sides hold their shape.

Before you can line the bag, you need to measure the bag's width (from side to side), height (from the turning ridge of the base to the turning ridge of the facing), and depth (the short side of the base).

The lining for this bag is not square, so it's a good idea to make a template for it. The width at the top of the bag is less than that at the bottom, so you need to make a template that is the height of your bag. Use the width measurement for the top edge of your template. The bottom edge of your template should measure the total of the width plus the depth. Thus, the sides of the template angle in from bottom to top.

Cut out two thicknesses of lining and interfacing using the template. Remember to add a ½" [1.3 cm] seam allowance when cutting the sides and the bottom of the lining (no seam allowance is needed for the top). Sandwich the lining such that the lining fabric is together, with RS facing each other and the interfacing on the outside. Sew around the three sides, forming a pocket, with an opening at the top. Press the seam allowances open. Shape the lining base into a rectangle by bringing the bottom corners of the pocket up onto the side seams and tacking them in place. To determine how high to position the corners, divide the bag's depth measurement in half. The resulting number is the level at which each corner should be positioned. For instance, if the depth of your bag is 6" [15 cm], position the bottom corners 3" [7.5 cm] up the side seam from the base. Sew the lining in place. Turn the bag right-side-out so the lining is inside the bag. Sew the top of the lining to the top edge of the bag (along the side of the turning ridge). Fold the bag facing over the raw edge of the lining and sew in place.

To help maintain the bag's shape at its base, make an insert by cutting a piece of stiff interfacing to size and, if desired, covering it by sewing on a sleeve of the lining fabric.

Handles

Use embroidery floss to sew handles to the bag and facing.

Molly's Amazing Technicolor Housecoat

Designer – Megan Curtis ☾
Pattern Rating – Nastily Exhausting Wizarding Test

Based on the house frock she wears in *Chamber of Secrets*, this sweater embodies the colorful spirit and kitschy charm of Molly Weasley, one of the most beloved characters in the Harry Potter series—and a magical knitter. The simple and sophisticated body is set off by outrageous yet gorgeous lace sleeves, which require both a strong personality to wear and an advanced knowledge of crochet techniques to make. True to Mrs. Weasley, this sweater is knit in a practical and economical soft cotton blend, so it is very washable, which will come in handy as you manage your Burrow's affairs.

Back

Using color A, CO 100 (110, 120) sts.

Work even in St st until piece measures 12½ (13, 13½)" [31.5 (33, 34.5) cm] or desired length from CO edge, ending with a WS row completed.

Armhole Shaping

BO 8 (9, 10) sts beg next 2 rows—84 (92, 100) sts.

Continue armhole shaping as follows:

Row 1 (RS): K2, ssk, knit to last 4 sts, k2tog, k2—82 (90, 98) sts.
Row 2 (WS): Purl.

Materials

☾ Knit Picks *Shine Worsted* (60% pima cotton, 40% modal, 75 yd. [68.5 m] per 50 g ball), #8061 Blush (color A), 9 (10, 12) balls, and Knit Picks *Shine Sport* (60% pima cotton, 40% modal, 110 yd. [100.5 m] per 50 g ball), #6555 Blush (color B), 2 skeins, #6556 River (color C), 2 skeins, #6557 Sky (color D), 3 skeins, #6560 Grass (color E), 2 skeins, #6561 Green Apple (color F), 2 skeins, #6565 Apricot (color G), 2 skeins, #6567 Butter (color H), 2 skeins, and #6568 Orchid (color I), 2 skeins

☾ Or yarn that knits to specified gauge: worsted-weight cotton- or wool-blend yarn, about 650 (735, 835) yd. [584 (672, 763) m] of color A, and sport-weight cotton-blend yarn, about 190 (195, 200) yd. [174 (178, 183) m] of colors B, C, E, and F; about 300 (310, 320) yd. [274 (284, 293) m] of color D; about 138 (148, 158) yd. [126 (135, 145) m] of color G; about 180 (185, 190) yd. [165 (169, 174) m] of color H; and about 167 (177, 187) yd. [153 (162, 171) m] of color I

☾ US 7 [4.5 mm] needles

☾ US G [4 mm] crochet hook

☾ Tapestry needle

☾ 6 buttons, 1⅛" [32 mm] in diameter.

Gauge

20 sts and 24 rows = 4" [10 cm] in St st using size 7 [4.5 m] needles and worsted-weight yarn

20 sts and 10 rows = 4" [10 cm] in dc using size G [4 mm] crochet hook and sport-weight yarn

Finished Size

M (L, XL)

To fit chest: 36 (40, 44)" [91.5 (101.5, 112) cm]

Chest circumference: 40 (44, 48)" [101.5 (112, 122) cm]

Length: 22 (23, 24)" [56 (58.5, 61) cm]

Sample shown: Size M

Note: This sweater, like Molly, is generously sized.

Stitch Guide for This Project

Stockinette Stitch (St st) Worked in Rows

Row 1 (RS): Knit.

Row 2 (WS): Purl.

Rep rows 1 and 2.

Note: This pattern uses many crochet techniques. For instructions on how to accomplish the basic crochet stitches, please see pages 158 and 159 in the appendix "Special Knitting Techniques."

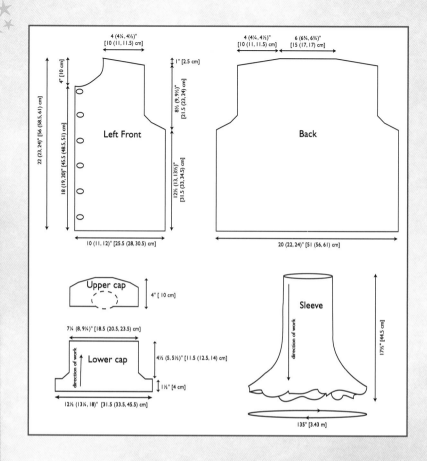

Rep last 2 rows 6 (7, 9) times more—70 (76, 80) sts.

Work even in St st until armhole measures 8½ (9, 9½)" [21.5 (23, 24) cm].

Shoulder Shaping

BO 7 (7, 8) sts beg next 2 rows—56 (62, 64) sts.

BO 7 (7, 8) sts beg next 2 rows—42 (48, 48) sts.

BO 6 (7, 7) sts beg next 2 rows—30 (34, 34) sts.

BO rem 30 (34, 34) sts for back neck.

Left Front

Using color A, CO 50 (55, 60) sts.

Work in St st until piece measures 12½ (13, 13½)" [31.5 (33, 34.5) cm] or desired length from CO edge, ending with a WS row completed.

Armhole Shaping

Begin armhole shaping as follows:

> **Next row (RS):** BO 8 (9, 10) sts, knit to end of row—42 (46, 50) sts.
>
> **Next row (WS):** Purl.

Continue armhole shaping as follows:

> **Row 1 (RS):** K2, ssk, knit to end of row—41 (45, 49) sts.
>
> **Row 2 (WS):** Purl.

Rep last 2 rows 6 (7, 9) times more—35 (38, 40) sts.

Work even until front measures 18 (19, 20)" [45.5 (48.5, 51) cm] from CO edge, ending with a RS row completed.

Neck Shaping

> **Next row (WS):** BO 7 (8, 8) sts at neck edge, purl to end of row—28 (30, 32) sts.

Continue neck shaping as follows:

> **Row 1 (RS):** Knit to last 4 sts, k2tog, k2—27 (29, 31) sts.
>
> **Row 2 (WS):** Purl.

Rep last 2 rows 7 (8, 8) times more—20 (21, 23) sts.

Work even in St st until armhole measures 8½ (9, 9½)" [21.5 (23, 24) cm], ending with a WS row completed.

Special Techniques for This Project

2-dc Cluster

[Yo, insert hook into next st, yo, and draw up a loop, yo and draw through 2 loops] in each of next 2 sts, yo and draw through all 3 loops on hook.

3-dc Cluster

[Yo, insert hook into next st, yo and draw up a loop, yo and draw through 2 loops] in each of next 3 sts, yo and draw through all 4 loops on hook.

5-dc Cluster

[Yo, insert hook into next st, yo and draw up a loop, yo, and draw through 2 loops] in each of next 5 sts, yo and draw through all 6 loops on hook.

5-tr Cluster

[Yo twice, insert hook into next st, yo and draw up a loop, (yo, draw through 2 loops) twice] in each of next 5 sts, yo and draw through all 6 loops on hook.

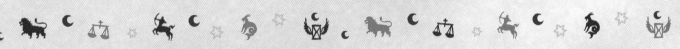

Stripe Pattern

Cap Top

E, F, H, B, C, F, G, F, I, C

Cap Bottom

Worked from 4 rnds below the armhole upward toward the cap top:

E, F, H, G, B, C, D, I, D, H, B, E, I, G

Sleeve

Worked from cap bottom to wrist:

I, B, D, H, C, E, F, I, G, B, F, D, E, F, H, G, C, F, G, I, B, C, E, F, I, G, I, B, H, E, D, C

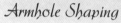

Shoulder Shaping

Shape shoulders as follows:

Row 1 (RS): BO 7 (7, 8) sts, knit to end of row—13 (14, 15) sts.

Row 2 (WS): Purl.

Rep last 2 rows once more—6 (7, 7) sts.

BO rem 6 (7, 7) sts.

Right Front

Using color A, CO 50 (55, 60) sts.

Work in St st until piece measures 12½ (13, 13½)" [31.5 (33, 34.5) cm] from CO edge, ending with a RS row completed.

Armhole Shaping

Begin armhole shaping as follows:

Next row (WS): BO 8 (9, 10) sts, purl to end of row—42 (46, 50) sts.

Next row (RS): Knit.

Continue armhole shaping as follows:

Row 1 (WS): P2, p2tog, purl to end of row—41 (45, 49) sts.

Row 2 (RS): Knit.

Rep last 2 rows 6 (7, 9) times more—35 (38, 40) sts.

Work even until front measures 18 (19, 20)" [45.5 (48.5, 51) cm] from CO edge, ending with a WS row completed.

Neck Shaping

Begin neck shaping as follows:

Next row (RS): BO 7 (8, 8) sts at neck edge, knit to end of row—28 (30, 32) sts.

Continue neck shaping as follows:

Row 1 (WS): Purl.

Row 2 (RS): K2, ssk, knit to end of row—27 (29, 31) sts.

Rep last 2 rows 7 (8, 8) times more—20 (21, 23) sts.

Work even in St st until armhole measures 8½ (9, 9½)" [21.5 (23, 24) cm], ending with a RS row completed.

Shoulder Shaping

Shape shoulders as follows:

> **Row 1 (WS):** BO 7 (7, 8) sts, purl to end of row—13 (14, 15) sts.
>
> **Row 2 (RS):** Knit.

Rep last 2 rows once more—6 (7, 7) sts.

BO rem 6 (7, 7) sts.

Sleeves

Note: To work the sleeves, start with the upper cap, working from the center out. Then work the lower cap section in rows, beginning several rows below the beginning of armhole shaping, proceeding upward toward the upper cap. This section is seamed to the upper cap later, after completion. Finally, work the sleeve from the lower cap down to the wrist, in rounds. When working the sleeves, it is much easier to weave in the ends as you go than to wait until the end. Believe me, you'll thank yourself later!

Upper Cap Section

Note: When instructed to join new yarn color, cut yarn of previous color, leaving 8" [20.5 cm] tail, and fasten off, unless instructed otherwise.

With color E and crochet hook ch 6 and join into rnd with sl st.

> **Rnd 1:** Ch 3, then work 14 dc into center of rnd, sl st to top of ch-3 to join—15 dc, including ch 3.
>
> **Rnd 2:** Join color F to top of ch-3 of previous rnd. Ch 2, sc in each dc, sl st to top of ch-2 to join—15 sc.
>
> **Rnd 3 (RS):** Join color H to top of 4th sc from ch-2. Ch 3, then work [1 dc in each sc] 11 times, leaving rem 4 sts unworked—12 dc, including ch-3. Do not turn work.

Note: From this point, you'll be working in rows, always joining new yarn at the far end and working with the RS facing.

> **Row 4 (RS):** Join color B to top of ch-3. Ch 3 then 1 dc in same st, work 2 dc in each dc—24 dc. Do not turn work.
>
> **Row 5:** Join color C to top of ch-3. Ch 4, *skip next st, 1 dc in next dc, ch 1, then dc into previous (skipped) dc, ch 1; rep from * 11 times more, dc into last dc—26 dc, including ch-3. Do not turn work.

Row 6: Join color F to 3rd ch of ch-4. Ch 3, work 2 dc into same st, *skip 2 sts, sc into next ch-1, skip 2 dc, 5dc into next ch-1; rep from * 4 times more, work 3 dc in last st—5 whole shells plus 2 half shells. Do not turn work.

Row 7: Join color G to top of ch-3. Ch 2, *skip 2 dc, 5 dc in next st, skip 2 dc, sc in next st (center of 5 dc in previous row); rep from * 5 times more, sc into last dc (top of last half shell)—6 shells. Do not turn work.

Row 8: Join color F to top of ch-2. Ch 3, work 2-dc cluster, ch 2, *sc into next st, work 5-dc cluster, ch 2; rep from * to end. Do not turn work.

Row 9: Join color I to top of ch-3. Ch 3, work 1 dc in each st to end of row. Turn work.

Row 10 (WS): Continuing with I, ch 3, work 1 dc in each dc to end of row. Turn work.

Row 11 (RS): Join color C to top of ch-3. Ch 3, work 1 dc in each dc to end of row.

Lower Cap Section

With color E ch 64 (68, 74).

Notes: You will be using the lower edge of this base ch later, when you begin working on the remaining lower part of the sleeve. Again, when instructed to join new yarn color, cut yarn of previous color, leaving an 8" [20.5 cm] tail, and fasten off, unless instructed otherwise. And always join new yarn at the far end and work with RS facing, unless otherwise instructed.

Row 1: Work 1 dc in 4th ch from end, 1 dc each ch to end—62 (66, 72) dc, including ch-3.

Row 2: Attach color F with sl st to top of ch-3. Ch 3, 1 dc in each dc to end.

Row 3: Attach color H with sl st to top of ch-3. Ch 3, 1 dc in each dc to end.

Row 4: Attach color G with sl st to top of ch-3. Ch 3, 1 dc in each dc to end of row.

Row 5: Attach color B with sl st to top of ch-3. Sl st across next 4 dc, sc in next st, 1 dc in next st and dc in each dc until 6 sts remain, dc in next st, sc in next st, sl st across rem 4 sts to end—54 (58, 64) sts.

Row 6: Attach color C with sl st to sc of previous row. Sl st across next 2 dc, sc in next st, 1 dc in next st, dc in each dc until 4 sts remain, sc in next st, sl st across remaining 3 sts—48 (52, 58) sts.

Row 7: Attach color D with sl st to sc. Ch 3, 1 dc in each dc across row, skip rem sc—46 (50, 56) sts.

Row 8: Attach color I with sl st to 2nd dc. Ch 3, 1 dc in each dc across row, skip last dc—44 (48, 54) sts.

Row 9: Attach color D with sl st to 3rd dc. Ch 3, 1 dc in each dc across row, skip last 2 dc—40 (44, 50) sts.

Row 10: Attach color H with sl st to 2nd dc. Ch 3, 1 dc in each dc across row, skip last dc—38 (42, 48) sts.

Row 11: Attach color B with sl st to 2nd dc. Ch 3, 1 dc in each dc across row, skip last dc—36 (40, 46) sts.

Row 12: Attach color E with sl st to 1st dc. Ch 3, 1 dc in each dc to end of row.

Row 13: Attach color I with sl st to 1st dc. Ch 3, 1 dc in each dc to end of row. Turn work.

Row 14: Continuing with color I, ch 3, 1 dc in each dc to end of row. Turn work for sizes L and XL and follow instructions below for L and XL.

For size M, continue with *All Sizes,* below.

Sizes L and XL Only

Row 15: Continuing with color I, ch 3, 1 dc in each dc to end. Turn work.

For size L, continue with *All Sizes,* below.

Size XL Only

Row 16: Continuing with color I, ch 3, 1 dc in each dc to end of row.

All Sizes

Rows 15 (16, 17): Cut yarn I and fasten off. Attach color G with sl st to 1st dc. Ch 3, 1 dc in each dc to end of row. Cut yarn and fasten off.

Weave in ends.

Place the circular portion of the cap top over the top of the last row [row 15 (16, 17)] of the lower cap so that it can be seen, the edges of the rem two side sections of the upper cap placed under the last row worked of the lower cap. With threaded tapestry needle, sew upper and lower caps together securely.

Sew side seams together.

Lower Cap to Wrist

With RS facing, turn the work upside-down, so the lower edge of the base ch is ready for you to begin the next rnd.

Note: Again, when instructed to join new yarn color, cut yarn of previous color, leaving 8" [20.5 cm] tail, and fasten off, unless instructed otherwise.

Rnd 1 (RS): Working across the lower edge of the base ch, attach color I with sl st to first ch (color E row of lower cap section). Ch 2 (for height only, do not count as st), 1 hdc in first ch, then hdc in each ch across, sl st to top of ch-2 to join in rnd—62 (66, 72) hdc.

Rnd 2: Attach color B with sl st to top of ch-2. Ch 3 (do not count as st), 1 dc in first hdc, then 1 dc in each hdc to end of rnd, sl st to top of ch-3 to join in rnd.

Rnd 3: Attach color D with sl st to ch-3. Ch 2, hdc first st, hdc in each dc to end of rnd, sl st to top of ch-2 to join in rnd.

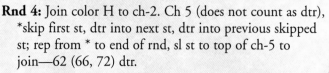

Rnd 4: Join color H to ch-2. Ch 5 (does not count as dtr), *skip first st, dtr into next st, dtr into previous skipped st; rep from * to end of rnd, sl st to top of ch-5 to join—62 (66, 72) dtr.

Rnd 5: Attach color C with sl st to ch-5. Ch 2 (does not count as hdc), 1 hdc in first st, hdc in each dtr to end of rnd, sl st to top of ch-2 to join in rnd—62 (66, 72) hdc.

Rnd 6: Attach color E with sl st to ch-2. Ch 3 (counts as 1 dc), work 1 (0, 0) dc into first st, then 1 dc in each hdc, sl st to top of ch-3 to join in rnd—63 (66, 72) dc including ch-3.

Rnd 7: Attach color F with sl st to ch-3. Ch 3 (does not count as st), *work 3-dc cluster, ch 3; rep from * to end of rnd, ch 3, sl st to top of beg ch-3 to join in rnd—21 (22, 24) clusters.

Rnd 8: Continuing with color F, ch 6, *work 3-dc cluster in next ch-3 space, ch 3; rep from * end of rnd, working last rep as 3-dc cluster in next ch-3 space, sl st to 3rd ch of ch-6 to join.

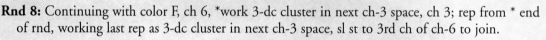

Rnd 9: Attach color I with sl st to 3rd ch of ch-6. Ch 4 (does not count as st), 1 tr in each st, *at the same time* increasing 2 (2, 0) sts evenly spaced to end, sl st to top of ch-4 to join in rnd—65 (68, 72) tr.

Rnd 10: Continuing with color I, ch 4, 1 tr in each st, *at the same time* increasing 1 (2, 0) sts evenly spaced to end, sl st to top of ch to join in rnd—66 (70, 72) tr.

Rnd 11: Continuing with color I, ch 4, 1 tr in each st, *at the same time* increasing 2 (2, 0) sts evenly spaced to end, sl st to top of ch to join in rnd—68 (72, 72) tr.

Rnd 12: Attach color G with sl st to ch-4. Ch 3, *skip 1 st, dc in next st, ch 1, dc in previous skipped st; rep from * to end of rnd, sl st to top of ch-3 join in rnd (1 dc in each st)—68 (72, 72) dc.

Rnd 13: Attach color B with sl st to ch-3. Ch 4, *skip 1 st, 3-dc shell in next st, skip 1 st, 1 dc in next st; rep from * to end of rnd, sl st to 3rd ch of ch-4 to join in rnd—17 (18, 18) shells.

Rnd 14: Attach color F with sl st to ch-3. Ch 4, *skip 1 st, 3-dc shell in next st, skip 1 st, 1 dc in next st; rep from * to end of rnd, sl st to 3rd ch of ch-4 to join in rnd.

Rnd 15: Attach color D with sl st to ch-3. Ch 4, *skip 1 st, 3-dc shell in next st, skip 1 st, 1 dc in next st; rep from * to end of rnd, sl st to 3rd ch of ch-4 to join in rnd.

Rnd 16: Attach color E with sl st to 3rd ch of ch-4. Ch 3 (does not count as st), *skip 2 sts, sc in next st, skip 2 sts, 5-dc shell in next st; rep from * to end of rnd, sl st to top of ch-3 to join in rnd—11 (12, 12) shells.

Rnd 17: Attach color F with sl st to ch-3. Ch 1, *ch 2, 5-dc cluster, ch 2, sc in next st; rep from * to end of rnd, sl st to ch 1 to join in rnd—11 (12, 12) clusters.

Rnd 18: Attach color H with sl st to ch-1. Ch 3, *skip 2 sts, sc in next st, skip 2 sts, 5-dc shell in next st; rep from * to end of rnd, sl st to ch-3 to join in rnd—11 (12, 12) shells.

Rnd 19: Attach color G with sl st to ch-3. Ch 1, *ch 2, 5-dc cluster, ch 2, sc in next st; rep from * to end of rnd, sl st to ch-1 to join—11 (12, 12) clusters.

Rnd 20: Continuing with color G, ch 1, *5 dc in joining st of cluster on row below, skip 2 sts, sc in next st; rep from * to end of rnd, sl st to ch-1 to join in rnd—11 (12, 12,) shells.

Rnd 21: Attach color C with sl st to ch-1. Sc in each st to end, sl st to ch-1 to join in rnd—66 (72, 72) sc.

Rnd 22: Continuing with color C, ch 4 (counts as 1 dc, ch 1), *skip next st, dc in next st, ch 1; rep from * to end of rnd, sl st to 3rd ch of ch-4 to join in rnd—66 (72, 72 sts).

Rnd 23: Attach color F with sl st to ch-3. Ch 1, *skip 2 sts, 5 tr in next st, skip 2 sts, sc in next st; rep from * to end of rnd, sl st to ch-1 to join in rnd—11 (12, 12) shells.

Rnd 24: Attach color G with sl st to ch-1. Ch 3, skip 1 st, sc in next st, *5 dc in next st, sc in next st, skip 1 st, 3 dc in next st, skip 1 st, sc in next st; rep from * to end of rnd, work last rep as 5 dc in next st, sc in next st, skip 1 st, 3 dc in next st, sl st to ch-3 to join in rnd—110 (120, 120) sts.

Rnd 25: Attach color I with sl st to ch-3. Ch 1, sc to end, sl st to ch-1 to join in rnd.

Rnd 26: Attach color B with sl st to ch-1. Ch 1, *skip 2 sts, 5 dc in next st, skip 2 sts, sc in next st, skip 1 st, 5 tr in next st, skip 1 st, sc in next st; rep from * to end of rnd, sl st to ch-1 to join in rnd—22 (24, 24) shells.

Rnd 27: Attach color C with sl st to center dc of dc-shell from previous pattern. Ch 4 (counts as 1 tr), *5-tr cluster, ch 3, sc in next st, ch 3; rep from * to end of rnd, sl st to top of ch-4 to join in rnd—22 (24, 24) clusters.

Rnd 28: Attach color E with sl st to top of ch-4. Ch 3 (counts as 1 dc), 4 dc in same st, *skip 2 sts, sc in next st, skip 2 sts, 5 dc next st; rep from * to end of rnd, sl st to top of ch-3 to join in rnd—30 (32, 32) shells.

Rnd 29: Attach color F with sl st to center of shell from previous rnd. *Ch 2, 5-dc cluster, ch 2, sc in next st; rep from * to end of rnd, sl st to top of ch-2 to join in rnd.

Rnd 30: Attach color I with sl st to ch-2. Ch 1, sc in each st increasing evenly across row to 248 sts for all sizes, sl st to ch-1 to join in rnd.

Rnd 31: Attach color G with sl st to ch-1. Ch 3, dc in each st, sl st to top of ch-3 to join in rnd.

Rnd 32: Attach color I with sl st to ch-3. Ch 1, sc in each st, sl st to ch-1 to join in rnd.

Rnd 33: Attach color B with sl st to ch-1. Ch 3 (counts as 1 dc), 1 dc in same st, 2 dc in each st to end, sl st to top of ch-3 to join in rnd—498 dc.

Rnd 34: Attach color H with sl st to ch-1. Ch 3 (counts as 1 dc), 4 dc in same st, *skip 2 sts, sc in next st, skip 2 sts, 5-dc shell in next st; rep from * to end of rnd, sl st to top of ch-3 to join in rnd—84 shells.

Rnd 35: Attach color E with sl st to center of shell from previous rnd. *Ch 2, 5-dc cluster, ch 2, sc in next st; rep from * to end of rnd, sl st to top of ch-2 to join in rnd.

Rnd 36: Attach color D with sl st to ch-2. Ch 4 (counts as 1 tr), 4 tr in same st, *skip 1 st, sc in next st, skip 1 st, 5 tr in next st; rep from * to end of rnd, sl st to top of ch-4 to join in rnd—135 shells.

Rnd 37: Attach color C with sl st to ch-4. Ch 1, loosely sc in each st, sl st to ch-1 to join in rnd. Cut yarn and fasten off.

Note: You might consider using a larger hook for rnd 37, the last rnd, to prevent curling.

Finishing

Weave in all rem ends.

Block sweater pieces to measurements, following yarn manufacturer's instructions.

Seam shoulders together with backstitch (see page 159) and seam sides together with mattress st (see page 160).

Space buttons evenly down left front and attach.

Starting at right side of front neck and using color F, sc all the way around neckline, then down left front, around bottom, and across the back. Continue sc up the right front, adding ch 7 loop for each buttonhole, coordinating each 7-ch loop with button positioning on left front.

Attach sleeves to armholes using backstitch, making sure to line up bottom of armhole to bottom of sleeve cap. Ease in extra sleeve cap fabric toward the top, making it slightly gathered, and seam flat section of lower cap.

Weave in all rem ends.

Materials

- Classic Elite *LaGran Mohair* (76.5% mohair, 17.5% wool, 6% nylon, 90 yd. [82 m] per 42 g ball): #6513 Black (yarn A), 1 ball, and Classic Elite *Inca Marl* (100% alpaca, 109 yd. [100 m] per 50 g skein): #1122 Nightingale (yarn B), 2 skeins

- Or any combination of yarns, from sport- to worsted-weight yarn, about 90 yd. [82 m] of yarn A and 175 yd. [160 m] of yarn B

- About 4 yd. [3.5 m] of scrap similar-weight yellow yarn for beak

- US 7 [4.5 mm] needles

- US 7 [4.5 mm] double-pointed needles

- Stitch markers

- Tapestry needle

- Polyfill stuffing

- 2 buttons, ⅝" [1.5 cm] in diameter

Gauge

16 sts and 20 rnds = 4" [10 cm] in St st using size 7 [4.5 mm] needles, with both yarns held together

Note: Gauge isn't important on this project. If you use thinner yarns, your owl will be a bit smaller; if you use thicker yarns, your owl will be a bit larger. Adjust the needle size to suit your yarn choice and just have fun with him!

ERROL

Designer – Andi Smith for knitbrit.com ☾ *Pattern Rating – Ordinary Wizarding Level*

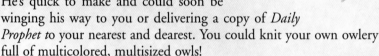

This furry little friend was inspired by Errol, the very tired, quite disheveled, but completely lovable old owl belonging to the Weasleys. As Errol is a bit of an odd bird, this project is an ideal way to use up odd balls of yarn tucked away in your stash. Try using fuzzy or loopy novelty yarns and stuff him unevenly for a wacky Errol truly worthy of the Weasleys. Or knit him in a beautiful feathery white yarn, stuff him fully, and turn him into Hedwig. He's quick to make and could soon be winging his way to you or delivering a copy of *Daily Prophet* to your nearest and dearest. You could knit your own owlery full of multicolored, multisized owls!

Instructions

Knitting begins at the bottom of the body and progresses up to the neck edge.

Body

Holding together one strand each of yarn A and yarn B, use the long-tail cast-on method to CO 16 sts.

Row 1 (and all other WS rows): Purl.

Row 2 (RS): K1f&b into each st—32 sts.

Row 4: Knit.

Row 6: K7, k1f&b, pm, k1f&b, k14, k1f&b, pm, k1f&b, k7—36 sts.

Row 8: *K to st before marker, k1f&b, slip marker, k1f&b; rep from * once more, k to end—40sts.

Rep the last 2 rows 2 times more—48 sts.

Work in St st until piece measures about 7" [18 cm], ending with a WS row.

Decrease as follows:

Row 1 (RS): Removing markers as you go, k1, k2tog, *k2, k2tog; rep from * to last st, k1—36 sts.

Row 2 (WS): Purl.

Row 3: K1, k2tog, *k2, k2tog; rep from * to last st, k1—27 sts.

BO purlwise.

Head

Work as for body through row 10—44sts.

Work 5 rows in St st, slipping markers as you go.

Decrease as follows:

Row 1 (RS): *Knit to 2 sts before marker, ssk, slip marker, k2tog; rep from * once more, knit to end—40 sts.

Row 2 (WS): Purl.

Finished Size

Height: approx 10" [25.5 cm]

Width: approx 5½" [14 cm]

Wingspan: approx 12" [30.5 cm]

Note: Size will vary depending on your yarn choice.

Stitch Guide for This Project

Stockinette Stitch (St st) Worked in Rows

Row 1 (RS): Knit.

Row 2 (WS): Purl.

Rep rows 1 and 2.

Special Techniques for This Project

I-cord

1. CO desired number of sts onto dpn or circular needle and knit across all sts.

2. Do not turn; instead, slide sts down to other end of needle and knit across all sts.

Rep step 2 until I-cord is desired length.

Rep the last 2 rows 2 times more—32 sts.

Next row: *K2tog; rep from * to end of row, removing markers as you go—16 sts.
Next row: Purl.

Cut yarn, leaving an 8" [20.5 cm] tail, and thread tail through rem sts to close top.

Base

Holding together one strand each of yarn A and yarn B, use the long-tail cast-on method to CO 16 sts.

Row 1 (RS): K1f&b, knit to last st, k1f&b—18 sts.
Row 2 (WS): Purl.

Rep the last 2 rows 3 times more—24 sts.

Decrease as follows:

Row 1: Ssk, knit to last 2 sts, k2tog—22 sts.
Row 2: Purl.

Rep the last 2 rows 3 times more—16 sts.

BO rem 16 sts.

Wings

Holding together one strand each of yarn A and yarn B, use the long-tail cast-on method to CO 7 sts.

Row 1 (WS): P1b&f, purl to last st, p1b&f—9 sts.
Row 2 (RS): Knit.

Rep the last 2 rows 2 times more—13 sts.

Beg with a purl row, work 5 rows even in St st.

Decrease as follows:

Row 1: Ssk, knit to last 2sts, k2tog—11 sts.
Rows 2–4: Beg with a purl row, work 3 rows even in St st.

Rep the last 4 rows 3 times more—5 sts.

Next row: Ssk, knit to last 2sts, k2tog—3 sts.
Next row: Sl 1, p2tog, psso—1 st.

Cut yarn, leaving an 8" [20.5 cm] tail, and thread tail through rem st.

Make second wing the same.

Talons

With dpn and one strand of yarn B, CO 6 sts.

Work 2" [5 cm] of I-cord for the leg.

Next row: K1f&b into each st and slide sts to opposite end of needle—12 sts.

Divide for talon toes:

Next row: Knit across first 4 sts only, holding rem 8 sts in reserve for other two toes.

With a third dpn, knit 1¼" [3 cm] I-cord. Cut yarn, leaving an 8" [20.5 cm] tail, thread through sts, and pull tightly.

Return to the dpn holding the 8 sts in reserve, join a new strand of yarn, and knit next 4 sts. Work I-cord for second talon toe and finish as for first. Rep with rem 4 sts on original dpn.

Working with each talon toe individually, thread the tail at the end of the toe through the center of the 4 st I-cord until it reaches the leg, thread through to the outside of the leg, and sew a stitch into the leg base so that the toe curls up a little. Thread the tail back to the inside of the leg. Run tail up through the center and cut. Rep for the rem 2 toes. Weave in the ends at the center of talon, closing the hole between the toes as you go. Leave the tail at the CO end of the leg intact for attaching to the body.

Make second talon the same.

Beak

Using a scrap of yellow yarn, CO 6 sts.

Row 1: K1f&b, knit to last st, k1f&b—8 sts.

Row 2: Purl.

Row 3: Rep row 1—10 sts.

Work in St st for 3 rows. Continuing in St st, BO 1 st each end every row until 2 sts remain.

Cut yarn, leaving an 8" [20.5cm] tail, thread through last 2 sts, and fasten off securely.

Finishing

Turn the body inside-out and, starting at the bottom, sew the seam along the center of the back, using mattress st (see page 160), up to about 2" [5 cm] from the top.

With RS together, sew the base onto the CO edge of the body. To position the base properly, the CO and BO edges (the two flat sides) of the base should be centered and aligned with the front and back of the body, and the two rounded edges of the base aligned with the sides of the bird. Turn right-side-out, loosely stuff the body with polyfill, and sew the rest of the back seam.

Turn the head inside-out and sew the seam at the center back. Turn right-side-out and gently stuff with polyfill. Matching back seams, attach the open part of the head to the body and sew securely.

Sew CO edge of each wing to one side of bird where head and body meet.

Attach the beak in the lower center of the head, sewing the edges of the beak together to close it into a cone shape, and weave in loose ends.

Using a long strand of yarn B, insert tapestry needle from the back of the neck through to about 1" [2.5 cm] on one side of the top of the beak. Thread one of the buttons on as an eye and sew down securely. Without cutting the yarn, move the needle through the head to the other side of the beak and attach the second button, then take the tapestry needle through the head and back down to the back of the neck. Tie a secure knot with both strands and fasten securely.

Weave in ends.

Note: Remember that Errol's anything but perfect; your owl will improve the more he is squished and rumpled.

Clock Blanket

Designer – Andi Smith for knitbrit.com C
Pattern Rating – Nastily Exhausting Wizarding Test

Materials

- Cascade *220 Superwash* (100% superwash wool, 220 yd. [201 m] per 100 g ball): #878 (color A), 5 balls, #813 (color B), 2 balls, #875 (color C), 2 balls, and #861 (color D), 3 balls
- Or similar yarn that knits to specified gauge: superwash wool or wool-blend yarn, about 1,000 yd. [914 m] of color A, 400 yd. [365 m] of color B, 400 yd. [365 m] of color C, and 600 yd. [550 m] of color D

Note: Depending on the amount of surface chain stitching you do, you may need more or less of colors C and D

- US 8 [5 mm] 40" [100 cm] circular needle

Note: It's fine to use a longer circular needle, but if you try to use a shorter one, your stitches won't fit comfortably on the cable.

- US 8 [5mm] double-pointed needles
- Stitch markers
- Tapestry needle
- Backing fabric (optional)
- Matching sewing thread (optional)
- Batting (optional)

Gauge

18 sts and 24 rows = 4" [10 cm] in St st using size 8 [5 mm] needles

Inspired by the clock in the Burrow that Molly Weasley uses to keep an eye on her family's whereabouts, this heirloom blanket will keep you cozy while tracking your clan. Worked in intarsia throughout, with chain stitch detail that adds a magical depth, the pattern may be more at Hermione's skill level than Neville's, but with some perseverance, you'll be the envy of Muggles and witches alike. The clock can be personalized easily by adding different destinations, more hands, people's names, beads, or other trim. Worked in a wonderful machine-washable wool, it's beautiful enough to hang on the wall, or you can add a fabric backing and toss it on the sofa.

Instructions

For each block of color in the central intarsia section, use a separate ball of yarn, unless the color block is 2 sts in width or less, in which case it is okay to carry yarn across these sts.

To keep yarns from tangling together, place each one in a zippered plastic bag and lay them out by your feet. As you come to a new color, twist the current yarn around the new yarn, always in the same direction. This anchors the color blocks and eliminates the need to sew them together.

Note: If you chose not to use the long-tail CO method, you must add one row of knit sts to the beginning of each block.

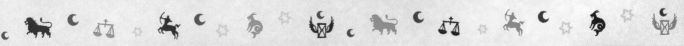

Finished Size

Width: 50" [127 cm]

Length: 48" [122 cm]

Stitch Guide for This Project

Stockinette Stitch (St st) Worked in Rows

Row 1 (RS): Knit.

Row 2 (WS): Purl.

Rep rows 1 and 2.

Reverse Stockinette Stitch Worked in Rows

Row 1 (RS): Purl.

Row 2 (WS): Knit.

Rep rows 1 and 2.

Special Techniques for This Project

8-Stitch I-cord

CO 8 sts onto one dpn.
1. With second dpn, knit these 8 sts. Do not turn.
2. Slide sts to other end of same needle.

Rep steps 1 and 2 until I-cord is desired length.

Center Panel

Using long-tail CO and color A, CO 180 sts.

Work 19 rows of St st, beginning with a purl row.

Next 180 rows: Continuing in St st, follow intarsia pattern in charts on pages 32–35.

Work 18 rows in St st, ending with a WS row completed.

BO all sts.

Top and Bottom Borders

Note: Borders consist of alternating St st and rev St st in colors D and A, interrupted by a large band of color B.

Using long-tail CO and color D, CO 180 sts.

Row 1 (RS): Purl.

Row 2 (WS): Knit.

Row 3: Knit.

Row 4: Switch to color A and purl.

Row 5: Knit.

Row 6: Purl.

Row 7: Switch to color D and knit.

Row 8: Knit.

Row 9: Purl.

Row 10: Knit.

Row 11: Knit.

Rows 12–14: Rep rows 4–6.

Rows 15–19: Rep rows 7–11.

Rows 20–22: Rep rows 4–6.

Rows 23–27: Rep rows 7–11.

Row 28: Switch to color B and purl.

Rows 29–36: Work 8 rows in St st, beginning with a knit (RS) row.

Rows 37–40: Rep rows 7–10.

BO all sts with color D.

Make second border the same.

Side Borders

Using long-tail CO and color D, CO 203 sts.

Row 1 (RS): P23, pm, p167, pm, p23.

Row 2 (WS): Knit.

Row 3: P3, k17, p3, slip marker, knit to next marker, p3, k17, p3.

Row 4: K3 with color D, p17 with color A, k3 with color D, slip marker, purl to marker with color A, slip marker, k3 with D, p17 with color A, k3 with color D.

Row 5: P3 with color D, k17 with color A, p3 with color D, slip marker, knit to marker with color A, slip marker, p3 with color D, k17 with color A, p3 with color D.

For rows 6–37, continue to work the 23 first and last sts as established in rows 4 and 5 while at the same time working the sts between the markers as for the top and bottom borders, beginning at row 6.

Row 38: Knit all sts with color D.

Row 39: Purl.

Row 40: Knit.

BO all sts with color D.

Make second side border the same.

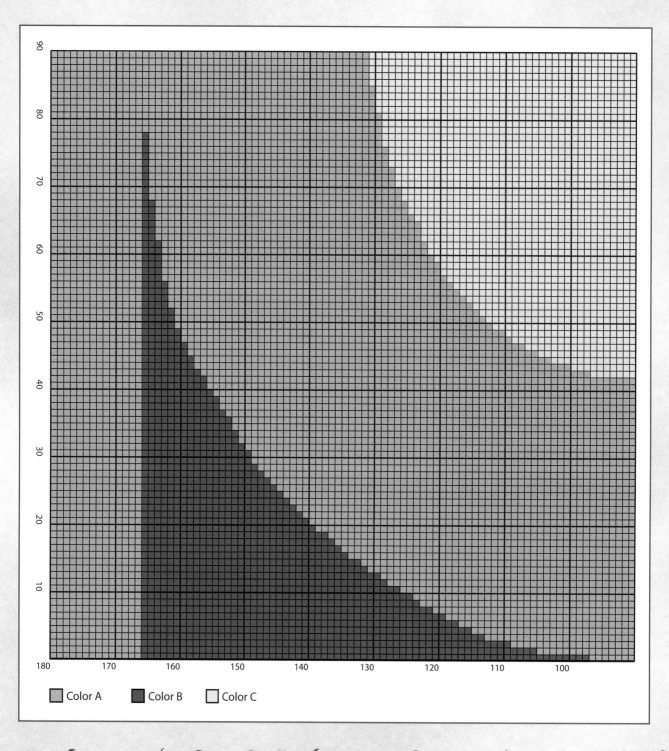

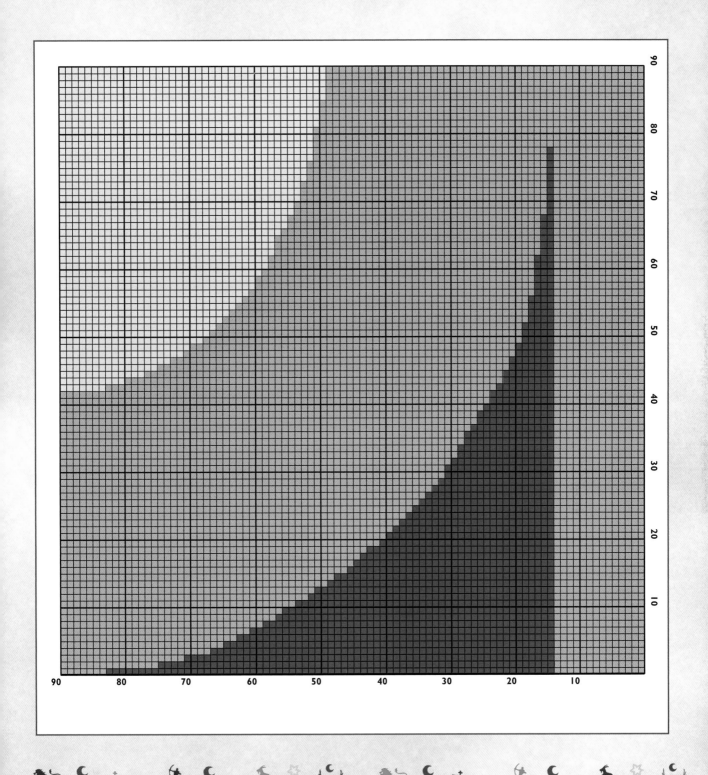

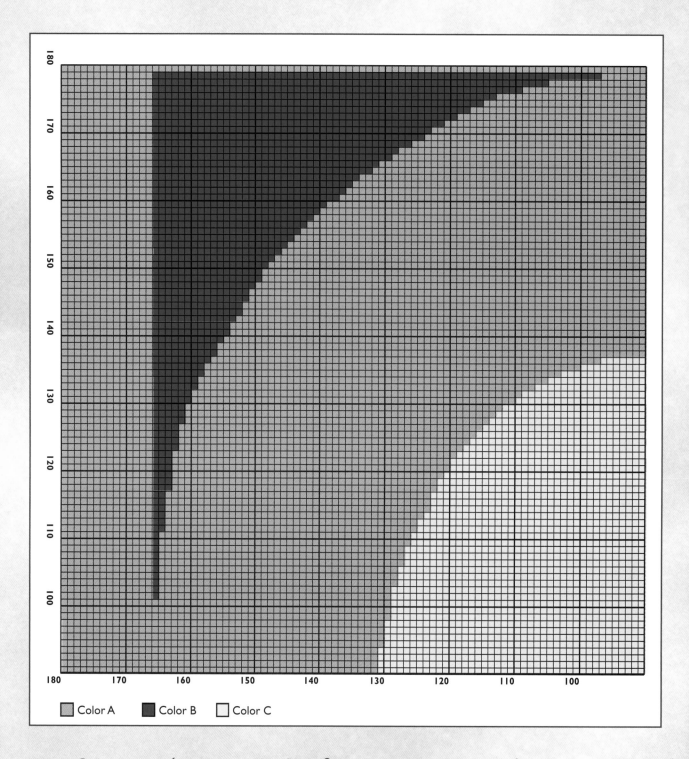

Color A   Color B   Color C

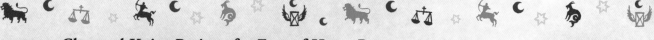

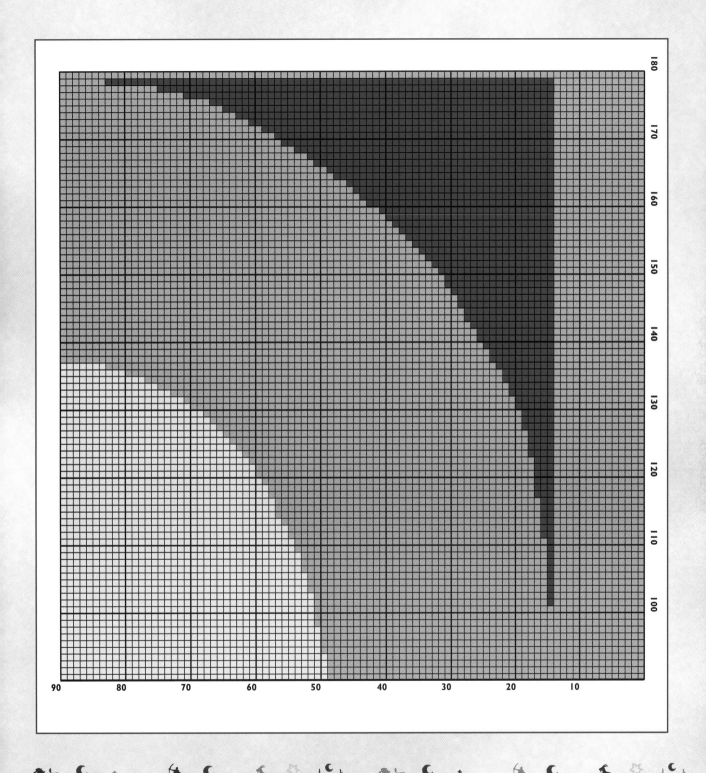

Hand(s)

With color D, CO 8 sts onto a dpn and work an I-cord 5" long, as described in the special techniques.

> **Row 1:** K1f&b, k6, k1f&b—10 sts.
> **Row 2 (and all other even rows):** Purl.
> **Row 3:** K1f&b, k8, k1f&b—12 sts.
> **Row 5:** K1f&b, k10, k1f&b—14 sts.

Work 5 rows in St st.

> **Next row:** Ssk, knit to last 2 sts, k2tog—12 sts.

Work 3 rows in St st.

Rep the last 4 rows 4 times more—4 sts.

> **Last row:** Sl 1, k3tog, psso—1 st.

Cut yarn, leaving an 8" [20.5 cm] tail, and thread tail through rem st.

Make as many more hands as you like.

Finishing

Note: The finishing instructions indicate where to sew chain sts on the surface of the work. If you prefer, you can work the chain sts using a crochet hook (see page 158). However, crocheted chains, in this case, will not have as flat a finished appearance as embroidered chains.

Lightly press the pieces into shape. Using matching colors of yarn and tapestry needle, seam the top and bottom borders to the center panel, then attach the side borders, making sure that seams and color blocks match. Weave in all lose ends behind matching color block.

Embroidery

Embroidered chain st (see page 157) around circle using color C. Each chain should be about the same size as a knitted st or a little larger.

Chain st along curved edge of blue shapes using color B.

On a piece of paper, trace around a plate about 8½" [21.5 cm] in diameter and cut out a template. Pin template onto center of blanket and, using color C, chain st around the template to form the center of the clock. Fold the paper circle template in half, in half again, and then once more to make eight equal sections. Use these as a guide to divide the center of the clock into eight equal sections. With a piece of

contrasting colored scrap yarn, baste a line extending each ray out from the plate edge to the blue border. Using color C, sew a single line of chain st along each of these eight rays from the center circle to the blue borders. Remove scrap yarn.

Place a pin every 1" [2.5 cm] along each ray. Using the pins as a guide, work two further rows of chain st in a braided pattern in color C, as follows: Starting in the center of the first chain st of a ray, and using the photo as a guide, chain 5 sts in a curve that ends at the next pin. Take the yarn *under* the straight ray and continue in chain st to the next pin, working the fifth chain st *over* the ray. Continue in this manner along the entire ray, working over and under the existing ray and removing the pins as you go. Work a second set of chain sts the same way as the first but beginning on the other side of the straight ray. Weave this line of chain sts by working them *over* the previous under stitch and *under* the previous over stitch when crossing the straight ray.

Using color C, work chain st in a straight line 1" [2.5 cm] inside the edge of the center panel all the way around. Then work the two braided rows described above around that straight chain.

With color D, use chain st to embroider the destinations in the eight clock sections. If you choose to follow the description in the books, use the following destinations: home, work, school, traveling, lost, hospital, prison, and mortal peril. To make sure each word is centered in its section, count how many letters are in the word and work the middle (or middle two) letters first, then each of the letters around them.

Note: It might be useful to use your computer to print the words out in a font of your choice; however, a freehand lettering style works very well and adds your own personal touch.

Weave in all ends.

Using color D, tack down the hand(s). If you wish to be able to move the hand(s) around from time to time, tack 1 stitch at the bottom of each hand, anchoring it to the center. This way, it will be able to move around much like the hand of a clock.

Backing and Batting (Optional)

If desired, add a fabric backing and batting. To add a fabric backing, measure the length and width of the blanket. You will need a piece of batting cut to the same measurements as the blanket and a piece of fabric 1" [2.5 cm] larger all around. *Note:* You should prewash and iron the fabric to avoid shrinkage or dye accidents.

Lay the blanket face down on a flat surface, ensuring that it is square at the corners and not stretched. Place the batting on top and then the fabric, face up, on top of the two layers. Pin all three layers securely, then turn the fabric edges between the batting and the blanket. Using the sewing thread, stitch the edges, making sure to go through all three layers. A running stitch, backstitch, or blanket stitch can be used.

Before removing the pins, using a large-eyed needle and coordinating yarn from the blanket, sew one stitch (in and out) of all three layers and tie securely on the back of the blanket every 6" [15 cm] or so throughout the blanket. This will anchor all three layers.

Diagon Alley

There's only one place to go to get all the things on your list from Hogwarts: Diagon Alley! It's got everything the young wizard needs—and needs to knit. These patterns come from all your favorite Diagon Alley shops, including a wizard cap and robe from Madame Malkin's, an exquisite invisibility shawl from Twillfit and Tattings, beautiful wand cozies from Ollivander's, and a jersey and socks from Quality Quidditch Supplies.

And don't forget, these items aren't just for young wizards going off to Hogwarts! There are adult sizes, too, so even Muggle parents can get in on the fun.

- Malabrigo *Merino Worsted* (100% wool; 215 yd. [196 m] per 3½ oz. hank): #195 Black, 1 (1, 2) hanks
- Or similar yarn that knits to specified gauge: worsted-weight wool or wool-blend yarn, about 165 (195, 235) yd. [150 (178, 215) m]
- US 6 [4 mm] 16" [40 cm] circular needle
- US 7 [4.5 mm] 16" [40 cm] circular needle
- US 7 [4.5 mm] double-pointed needles
- Stitch marker
- Tapestry needle
- 2 yd. [1.83 m] feather-light boning strip (available at sewing/fabric store; optional)
- Sewing needle (optional)
- Black sewing thread (optional)

Gauge

20 sts and 26 rnds = 4" [10 cm] in St st using size 7 [4.5 mm] needles

Finished Size

S (M, L)

Circumference: 19½ (21½, 23½)" [49.5 (54.5, 59.5) cm]

Length: 13 (13½, 14)" [33 (34.5, 35.5) cm]

Sample shown: Size S

Stitch Guide for This Pattern

Stockinette Stitch (St st) Worked in Rounds

Knit all sts.

STUDENT WIZARD CAP

Designer – Alison Hansel ☾ *Pattern Rating – First Year*

Every student at Hogwarts gets one! You can wear this tall, pointed hat like a floppy stocking cap or add the flexible boning to help it magically stand up on your head, just like the students' hats in the films. Knit in a super-soft and lightweight merino wool, this hat is comfortable enough to be a part of your everyday uniform and perfect for tossing in the air when your school wins the House Cup!

Instructions

With smaller circ needle, CO 100 (110, 120) sts, pm to note beg rnd, and join in a circle, being careful not to twist sts.

Brim

Work 12 rnds in St st. Purl next rnd to form turning ridge. Work 12 more rnds in St st.

Fold the first 12 rnds of hat to inside to make hem, leaving single purl rnd as bottom edging and lining up CO edge with sts on needle. Knit each st of the next rnd together with 1 st from CO edge.

Switch to larger circ needle and continue working in St st until piece measures 3½ (4, 4½)" [9 (10, 11.5) cm] from turning ridge.

Work Decreases

Note: When you have too few sts to continue working on the circular needle, switch to dpns.

Next rnd: *K8, k2tog; rep from * to end of rnd—90 (99, 108) sts.

Knit 6 rnds without decreasing.

Next rnd: *K7, k2tog; rep from * to end of rnd—80 (88, 96) sts.

Knit 6 rnds without decreasing.

Next rnd: *K6, k2tog; rep from * to end of rnd—70 (77, 84) sts.

Knit 6 rnds without decreasing.

Next rnd: *K5, k2tog; rep from * to end of rnd—60 (66, 72) sts.

Knit 6 rnds without decreasing.

Next rnd: *K4, k2tog; rep from * to end of rnd—50 (55, 60) sts.

Knit 6 rnds without decreasing.

Next rnd: *K3, k2tog; rep from * to end of rnd—40 (44, 48) sts.

Knit 6 rnds without decreasing.

Next rnd: *K2, k2tog; rep from * to end of rnd—30 (33, 36) sts.

Knit 6 rnds without decreasing.

Next rnd: *K1, k2tog; rep from * to end of rnd—20 (22, 24) sts.

Knit 6 rnds without decreasing.

Next rnd: *K2tog; rep from * to end of rnd—10 (11, 12) sts.

Knit 6 rnds without decreasing.

Next rnd: K0 (1, 0), *k2tog; rep from * to end of rnd—5 (6, 6) sts.

Finishing

Cut yarn, leaving an 8" [20.5 cm] tail, and thread tail through rem sts to close top of hat. Weave in ends.

Block, if desired, according to yarn manufacturer's instructions.

Add Boning (Optional)

If desired, cut three or four strips of boning about ½" [1.3 cm] shorter than length of hat. Turn hat inside-out. With black sewing thread, whipstitch each boning strip vertically to the inside of the hat, spacing them evenly apart. Turn hat right-side-out again.

Materials

- Lion Brand *Wool-Ease* (80% acrylic, 20% wool; 197 yd. [180 m] per 85 g ball): #620-153 Black, 7 (13, 17) balls
- Or similar yarn that knits to specified gauge: worsted-weight wool or wool-blend yarn, about 1,300 (2,550, 3,350) yd. [1,190 (2,330, 3,050) m]
- US 9 [5.5 mm] 24" [60 cm] or longer circular needle
- One straight or double-pointed needle for three-needle bind-off
- US G [4.25 mm] crochet hook
- Tapestry needle
- Stitch markers
- Stitch holders
- 2 round black shank buttons (or more, in pairs, if you wish to button the full length of the robe)

Gauge

17 sts and 23 rows to = 4" [10 cm] in St st using size 9 [5.5 mm] needles

Finished Size

S (M, L)

To fit chest up to 28 (32, 36)" [71 (82, 91.5) cm]

Finished chest circumference: 30½ (35½, 39¼)" [77.5 (90, 99.5) cm]

Length (from neck to hem): 35 (45, 48)" [89 (114.5, 122) cm]

Sample shown: Size S

WIZARD ROBE

Designer – Heather Brack ☾ *Pattern Rating – Ordinary Wizarding Level*

To protect your house sweater from potion spills and accidental explosions, it is recommended that you wear a robe to class. This hand-knit version has a full, warm hood to protect your ears from the wind on the long walk to Care of Magical Creatures class or during Quidditch matches. The sleeves are very full but should not come too far past the wrist, to avoid being dragged through your cauldron. But just in case, the yarn is completely machine washable and much easier to care for than those Blast-Ended Screwts!

Back

CO 103 (133, 161) sts.

Work in moss st, as described in the stitch guide, for 6 rows.

Changing to St st, beg with a WS row, and work decreases as follows.

Decreases

Note: When working decreases, work k2tog on the RS or p2tog on the WS.

Dec 4 sts, evenly spaced, across every 18th (14th, 10th) row 5 (10, 15) times—83 (93, 101) sts.

Dec 1 st at each edge on every following 8th (7th, 7th) row 8 times— 67 (77, 85) sts.

Work even until piece measures 29 (36, 38½)" [73.5 (91.5, 98) cm] from CO edge, ending with a WS row completed.

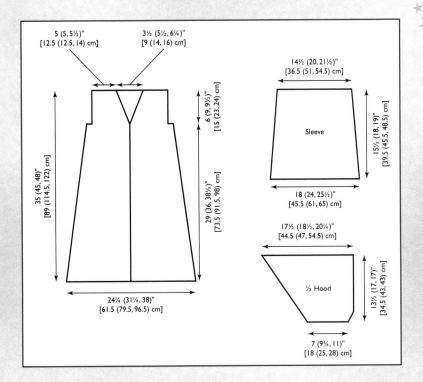

Moss Stitch Worked in Rows over an Odd Number of Sts

Row 1: *K1, p1; rep from * to last st, k1.

Rep row 1.

Stockinette Stitch (St st) Worked in Rows

Row 1 (RS): Knit.

Row 2 (WS): Purl.

Rep rows 1 and 2.

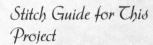

Armhole Shaping

BO 5 sts beg next 2 rows—57 (67, 75) sts.

Work even until armhole measures 6 (9, 9½)" [15 (23, 24) cm] from armhole BO.

Place all sts on holder.

Right Front

CO 51 (67, 81) sts.

Work in moss st for 6 rows.

Row 7 (WS): Purl to last 5 sts, work 5 sts in moss st.
Row 8 (RS): Work first 5 sts in moss st, knit to end.

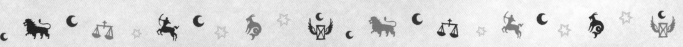

Decreases

Continuing to work 5 sts in moss st along center front edge while working the rest of the row in St st, dec as follows:

Dec 2 sts evenly spaced across St st section every 18th (14th, 10th) row 5 (10, 15) times—41 (47, 51) sts.

Dec 1 st at side (non-moss st) edge every 8th (7th, 7th) row 8 times—33 (39, 43) sts.

Work even, continuing to work 5 sts at center front edge in moss st and rest of piece in St st, until piece measures 29 (36, 38½)" [73.5 (91.5, 98) cm] from CO edge, ending with a RS row completed.

Armhole and Neck Shaping

Next row (WS): BO 5 sts, purl to last 5 sts, work 5 sts in moss st—28 (34, 38) sts.

Next row (RS): Work first 5 sts in moss st, k2tog, knit to end.

Next 3 rows: Work even, continuing to work 5 sts at center front edge in moss st and rest of piece in St st.

Rep last 4 rows 6 (11, 13) times more to form v-neck—21 (22, 24) sts.

Work even, continuing to work 5 sts at center front edge in moss st and rest of piece in St st, until armhole measures 6 (9, 9½)" [15 (23, 24) cm].

Place all sts on holder.

Left Front

CO 51 (67, 81) sts.

Work in moss st for 6 rows.

Row 7 (WS): Work 5 sts in moss st, purl to end.

Row 8 (RS): Knit to last 5 sts, work 5 sts in moss st.

Decreases

Work decreases as for right front (see page 44)—33 (39, 43) sts.

Work even, continuing to work 5 sts at center front edge in moss st and rest of piece in St st, until piece measures 29 (36, 38½)" [73.5 (91.5, 98) cm] from CO edge, ending with a WS row completed.

Armhole and Neck Shaping

Next row (RS): BO 5 sts, knit to last 5 sts, work 5 sts in moss st—28 (34, 38) sts.

Work 1 row even.

Next row (RS): Knit to last 7 sts, ssk, work 5 sts in moss st.

Next 3 rows: Work even, continuing to work 5 sts at center front edge in moss st and rest of piece in St st.

Rep last 4 rows 6 (11, 13) times more to form v-neck—21 (22, 24) sts.

Work even, continuing to work 5 sts at center front edge in moss st and rest of piece in St st, until armhole measures 6 (9, 9½)" [15 (23, 24) cm].

Join Shoulders

For each shoulder, move back and front sts from stitch holders onto needles. With a third needle, join each shoulder using three-needle bind-off (see page 161).

Sleeves

CO 61 (85, 91) sts.

Working in St st, inc 1 st at each side every 10th row 8 (8, 9) times—77 (101, 109) sts.

Work even until piece measures 14½ (17, 18)" [37 (43, 45.5) cm] from CO edge.

Work 6 rows in moss st.

BO all sts in patt.

Make second sleeve the same.

Lapels

Right Lapel

Starting at the top edge of the right front neck, with WS facing, pick up and p19 (25, 27) sts down the v-neck. Turn.

Note: See page 157 for instructions on how to pick up and purl.

Row 1 (RS): BO 1, knit to end—18 (24, 26) sts.

Row 2 (WS): Knit to last 2 sts, k2tog—17 (23, 25) sts.

Row 3: P2tog, purl to end—16 (22, 24) sts.

Rep last 2 rows 5 (6, 7) times more, then work row 2 once more—5 (9, 9) sts.

Last row: P2tog, BO rem sts.

Left Lapel

Starting at the top edge of the left neck, with RS facing, pick up and k19 (25, 27) sts down the v-neck and turn.

Row 1 (WS): BO 1, purl to end—18 (24, 26) sts.

Row 2 (RS): Purl to last 2 sts, p2tog—17 (23, 25) sts.

Row 3: K2tog, knit to end—16 (22, 24) sts.

Rep last 2 rows 5 (6, 7) times more, then work row 2 once more—5 (9, 9) sts.

Last row: K2tog, BO rem sts.

Hood

Beg at edge of right front, with RS facing, pick up and k11 (15, 17) sts across the top of the right lapel, pick up and k15 (23, 27) sts across the back of the neck, and pick up and k11 (15, 17) sts across the top of the left lapel—37 (53, 61) sts.

Row 1 (WS): Purl.

Row 2 (RS): Kf&b of first 11 (15, 17) sts, knit across back neck sts to opposite lapel, kf&b of last 11 (15, 17) sts—59 (83, 95) sts.

Row 3 (WS): Sl 1, [k1, p1] 3 times, pm, purl to last 7 sts, pm, [p1, k1] 3 times, k1.

Row 4 (RS): Sl 1, [k1, p1] 3 times, slip marker, knit to other marker, slip marker, [p1, k1] 3 times, k1.

Row 5: Sl 1, [k1, p1] 3 times, slip marker, purl to other marker, slip marker, [p1, k1] 3 times, k1.

Row 6: Work 7 border sts as established, slip marker, k7 (7, 8), [m1, k4] 9 (15, 17) times, knit to other marker, slip marker, work last 7 border sts as established—68 (98, 112) sts.

Row 7: Rep row 5, placing a third marker after working 34 (49, 56) sts.

Row 8: Work 7 border sts, slip marker, m1, knit to 1 st before center marker, m1, k1, slip marker, k1, m1, knit to last marker, m1, slip marker, work 7 border sts—72 (102, 116) sts.

Row 9: Rep row 5, slipping all markers.

Rep last 2 rows 4 times more—88 (118, 132) sts.

Row 18: Work 7 border sts, slip marker, knit to 1 st before center marker, m1, k1, slip marker, k1, m1, knit to last marker, slip marker, work 7 border sts—90 (120, 134) sts.

Row 19: Rep row 9.

Row 20 (sizes M and L *only*): Work 7 border sts, slip marker, knit to last marker, work 7 border sts.

Row 21 (sizes M and L *only*): Rep row 9.

Rep last 2 (4, 4) rows (increasing on either side of the center marker only every 2nd [4th, 4th] row) 29 (19, 19) times more—148 (158, 172) sts.

Divide sts evenly between 2 needles and, with RS together, use a third needle to work three-needle bind-off (see page 161) across sts.

Finishing

Using invisible vertical-to-horizontal seam (see page 160), sew sleeves into armholes, beginning at the shoulder seam and working down each side. Using mattress stitch (see page 160), sew side and sleeve seams. Weave in all rem ends.

Using crochet hook, ch10 (or more or fewer, as required to fit around your buttons) and join first chain to last to form a loop. Make a loop for each button on your robe.

If using a single pair of buttons, sew the top button about 1" [2.5 cm] below the bottom of the v-neck. Sew the second button about ½" [1.5 cm] below the first. Position button loops on opposite side and stitch securely in place. If you are making your robe to button all the way down the front, continue spacing pairs of buttons evenly down the length of the robe.

Block according to yarn manufacturer's instructions, paying particular attention to the moss st borders, which may tend to fold inward.

Materials

- Hip Knits *Laceweight Cashmere* (100% hand-dyed cashmere, 1,640 yd. [1,500 m] per 70 g skein), Pale Gray, 1 skein
- Or similar yarn that knits to specified gauge: laceweight luxury fiber, about 850 (1,300) yd. [779 (1,189) m]
- US 7 [4.5 mm] needles
- US 10 [6 mm] needles
- Stitch markers
- Tapestry needle

Gauge

Before blocking: 29 sts and 32 rows = 4" [10 cm] in patt using size 7 [4.5 mm] needles

After blocking: 20 sts and 28 rows = 4" [10 cm] in patt using size 7 [4.5 mm] needles

Finished Size (After Blocking)

S (L)

Width: 16 (25)" [40.5 (63.5) cm]

Length: 50" [127 cm] or desired length

Sample shown: Size S

INVISIBILITY SHAWL

Designer – Kerrie Allman ☾ *Pattern Rating – Ordinary Wizarding Level*

A light and airy lace shawl inspired by Harry's invisibility cloak. Knit in a pale gray hand-dyed cashmere, it provides an almost invisible layer of warmth in a fiber as luxurious as the rare materials the wizarding world uses to make the cloaks. The lace pattern is quite simple, and there's no shaping, so this shawl would be a terrific first lace project for the adventurous beginning knitter.

Instructions

Note: To keep the edges flexible enough to stretch as the shawl is blocked, special cast-on and bind-off techniques are used.

Using the provisional cast-on method (see page 155), CO 80 (128) sts, leaving a tail about 60 (100)" [152 (254) cm] long, to bind off the CO edge later.

With larger needles, knit 2 rows in garter st, as described in the stitch guide.

Change to smaller needles and work 4 rows more in garter st.

Beg with row 1, work lace patt as described in the stitch guide until work measures about 40" [101.5 cm], or about 10" [25.5 cm] shorter than desired length, ending with row 3 of lace patt completed.

Work 5 rows in garter st.

Change to larger needles and knit 1 row.

Cut yarn, leaving a tail about 60 (100)" [152 (254) cm] long for binding off.

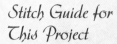

Finishing

Slip live sts onto scrap yarn twice the length of the shawl's width and tie scrap yarn ends together to prevent sts from escaping.

Block shawl by soaking in tepid water and then squeezing gently to remove excess water. Pin shawl to finished size measurements indicated or to desired measurements and allow to dry. When shawl is dry, return live sts to larger needle and BO with long tail, using ssk BO (see page 154).

Remove provisional CO, slipping sts onto larger needle. Using the long attached yarn tail, BO sts using ssk BO.

Weave in ends.

Stitch Guide for This Project

Garter Stitch Worked in Rows

Knit every row.

Lace Pattern Worked in Rows

Rows 1 and 3: K4, *k1, yo, k4, sl 1, k2tog, psso, k4, yo; rep from * to last 4 sts, k4.

Row 2: K4, purl to last 4 sts, K4.

Row 4: Knit.

Rep rows 1–4.

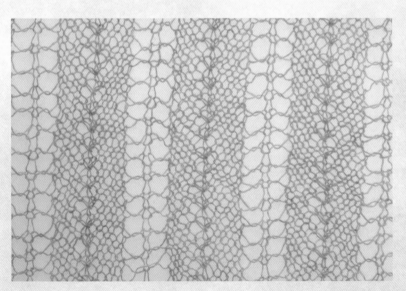

A pair of sophisticated and charming cases for stashing your wand or, in your Muggle moments, your knitting needles. There's a beautiful but simple unicorn case and a more complex dragon skin patterned case, each knit in lovely yarns reminiscent of the magical creatures of the wizarding world.

Fleur's Faux Unicorn Wand Clutch

Unicorns are beloved for their beauty almost as much as their powerful magic. That makes this horn-shaped clutch knit from spun Muggle silk that strongly resembles the fine, luminescent hair of a unicorn the perfect carrying case for your magic wand. This clutch is knit flat from the top down, beginning with a picot edging.

Instructions

CO 33 sts loosely.

Note: A backward loop or provisional cast-on (see page 155) works well here.

Beg with a knit row, work 6 rows in St st.

> **Next row (picot row):** K1, *yo, k2tog; rep from * to end of row—33 sts.

Work 5 rows in St st.

Fold the piece along the picot row, with WS together, so that the CO edge is lined up with the live sts. In the next row, knit each st by passing the right needle through the st as if to knit then through a loop on the CO edge and knitting these 2 sts together. Continue in this manner across the row, joining the leading edge to the CO edge. This creates both a picot edging and a casing for the drawstring.

> **Rows 1–4:** Work in St st.
>
> **Row 5 (dec row):** K1, k2tog, knit to last 3 sts, ssk, k1.

Materials for Fleur's Faux Unicorn Wand Clutch

- ☾ Tilli Tomas *Rock Star* (100% silk with glass beads, 150 yd. [137 m] per 100 g hank), White, 1 hank
- ☾ Or similar yarn that knits to specified gauge: DK-weight or light worsted silk or silk-blend yarn, about 55 yd. [50 m] yarn without beads
- ☾ US 4 [3.5 mm] needles
- ☾ Tapestry needle
- ☾ Less than ¼ yd. [23 cm] of silver/blue lining fabric
- ☾ Thread
- ☾ Sewing needle
- ☾ Size E [3.5 mm] crochet hook

Gauge

22 sts and 23 rows = 4" [10 cm] in St st using size 4 [3.5 mm] needles

Finished Size

Width at top: 3½" [9 cm]

Length: 14" [35.5 cm]

Stitch Guide for This Pattern

Stockinette Stitch (St st) Worked in Rows

Row 1: Knit.

Row 2: Purl.

Rep rows 1 and 2.

Rep last 5 rows 13 times more—5 sts rem.

Work 4 rows in St st.

Cut yarn, leaving a 36" [91.5 cm] tail, and thread tail through rem sts twice, then draw closed.

Finishing

Remove the beads from the yarn tail and use the tail to sew the back seam, using mattress stitch (see page 160), leaving the 5 rows before the picot row open to allow the drawstring to pass through. Block according to yarn manufacturer's instructions, with the seam positioned along the center back, and allow to dry thoroughly. Weave in all rem ends.

Lining

Trace and cut a triangle of lining fabric the same length as and twice the width of the finished case. Fold the fabric in half, and using backstitch or a sewing machine, seam the two long edges together, leaving about a ¼" [6 mm] seam allowance. Turn over about ½" [1.3 cm] of fabric at the top edge, toward the outside. Use a knitting needle (or magic wand) to slip the lining into the case, with RS of lining facing inside, and the turned-over edge facing the WS of knitting. Stitch the top edge of the lining into the knit piece just below the CO edge and edging seam, using thread and an overcast stitch.

Drawstring

Using crochet hook, make a crochet chain (see page 158) about 16" [40.5 cm] long, or desired length, to serve as a drawstring. Tie a knot at each end of the chain to secure the ends.

Thread tapestry needle with the crochet drawstring, or attach drawstring to a safety pin or bodkin and draw through the casing, inserting the drawstring through one opening below the picot edge and exiting out the other on the opposite side.

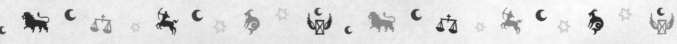

Materials for Bill's Dragon Skin Wand Case

- Louet *Euroflax Sport Weight* (100% linen, 270 yd. [246 m] per 100 g hank), #2934 Jungle Green, 1 hank
- Or similar yarn that knits to specified gauge: DK-weight linen or cotton yarn, about 75 yd. [68.5 m]
- US 5 [3.75 mm] needles
- Tapestry needle
- Less than ¼ yd. [23 cm] canvas or cotton duck fabric in a matching color
- Thread
- Sewing needle

Gauge

24½ sts and 29 rows = 4" [10 cm] in dragon st using size 5 [3.75 mm] needles

Finished Size

Width: 3" [7.5 cm]

Length: 15½" [39 cm]

Bill's Dragon Skin Wand Case

This dragon skin wand case was a gift from Bill Weasley's dragon-expert brother Charlie. It's tough enough to protect the contents from many mishaps, and the optional belt loop allows it to be worn at your side, like a holster. The sample shown here is a Welsh Green dragon.

Instructions

CO 37 sts. Purl 1 row (this is a WS row).

Beg working dragon st, using either the chart or the stitch guide on page 53. Work rows 1–8 12 times (96 rows total), then shape point, beg with row 97, as follows:

Row 97: K1, *ssk, k2, k2tog, k2, m1, k1, m1, k2, ssk, k2, k2tog, k1; rep from * to end of row—33 sts.

Row 98 (and all other even-numbered rows): Purl.

Row 99: K1, *ssk, k2tog, k3, m1, k1, m1, k3, ssk, k2tog, k1; rep from * to end of row—29 sts.

Row 101: K1, *ssk, k2, k2tog, m1, k1, m1, ssk, k2, k2tog, k1; rep from * to end of row—25 sts.

Row 103: K1, *ssk, k2tog, k1, m1, k1, m1, k1, ssk, k2tog, k1; rep from * to end of row—21 sts.

Row 105: K1, *ssk, k5, k2tog, k1; rep from * to end of row—17 sts.

Row 107: K1, *ssk, k3, k2tog, k1; rep from * to end of row—13 sts.

Row 109: K1, *ssk, k1, k2tog, k1; rep from * to end of row—9 sts.

Row 111: K1, *sl 1, k2tog, psso, k1; rep from * to end of row—5 sts.

Row 113: Ssk, k1, ssk—3 sts.

Cut yarn, leaving an 8" [20.5 cm] tail, and draw through rem sts.

Finishing

Belt Loop (Optional)

CO 12 sts. Work in moss st as described in the stitch guide (see page 53) until piece measures 2" [5 cm] in length, or ½" [1.3 cm] longer than belt width. BO sts in patt.

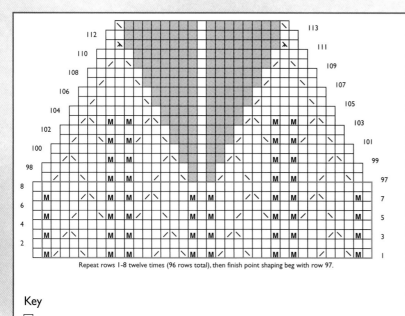

Repeat rows 1–8 twelve times (96 rows total), then finish point shaping beg with row 97.

Key

☐ Knit on RS; purl on WS

☑ k2tog—Knit 2 sts together (single left-leaning decrease)

◩ ssk—Sl 2 sts one at a time, knitwise, from left needle to right needle, insert left needle tip into front of both slipped sts and knit them together from this position (single right-leaning decrease)

⋏ Sl 1 kwise, k2tog, psso (double decrease)

Ⓜ m1 (make 1)— Insert left needle tip from front to back under the running strand between both needles, insert right needle tip into back strand and knit to make 1 st (makes an increase between 2 sts)

▨ No stitch—These squares help maintain the shape of the chart; ignore them and work the next st as shown

☐ Pattern repeat frame

Recommended Colors for Other Dragons

Swedish Short-Snout: Louet *Euroflax Sport Weight* #2824 Great Lakes

Chinese Fireball: Louet *Euroflax Sport Weight* #2114 Red

Hungarian Horntail: Louet *Euroflax Sport Weight* #2224 Black

Stitch Guide for This Pattern

Dragon St (Worked over 37 Sts)

Setup row (WS): Purl.

Row 1 (RS): *K1, m1, ssk, k2, k2tog, k2, m1, k1, m1, k2, ssk, K2, k2tog, m1; rep from * to last st, k1.

Rows 2, 4, 6, and 8 (WS): Purl.

Row 3: *K1, m1, k1, ssk, k2tog, k3, m1, k1, m1, k3, ssk, k2tog, k1, m1; rep from * to last st, k1.

Row 5: *K1, m1, k2, ssk, k2, k2tog, m1, k1, m1, ssk, k2, k2tog, k2, m1; rep from * to last st, k1.

Row 7: *K1, m1, k3, ssk, k2tog, k1, m1, k1, m1, k1, ssk, k2tog, k3, m1; rep from * to last st, k1.

Rep rows 1–8.

Moss St Worked in Rows Over Even Number of Sts

Row 1 (RS): *K1, p1; rep from * to end of row.

Row 2 (WS): *P1, k1; rep from * to end of row.

Rep rows 1 and 2.

Blocking

Block according to yarn manufacturer's instructions and dry flat.

Lining

Cut a rectangle of fabric 5" [12.5 cm] wide and 15" [38 cm] long. Fold in half and trim one end to match the point at the bottom of the knitted piece.

Sew the point and long open side of the fabric lining, leaving about a ¼" [6 mm] seam allowance. Turn over the top ½" [1.3 cm] edge. Place lining so that the WS of the lining is facing the WS of the knitted piece. Fold the knitted case around the lining so that the top edge of the lining is ½–¾" [1.3–2 cm] below the top of the knitting and the lower points of lining and knitting are roughly aligned. (The lining point should end about ½" [1.3 cm] before the point of the knit fabric.) Whipstitch the lining top edge in place.

Starting from the point, sew the long side of the knitted piece closed, using mattress stitch (see page 160). Weave in all rem ends.

If you made a belt loop, position it about 2" [5 cm] below the top edge, or as desired, and sew the top and bottom loop edges carefully, using whipstitch.

Materials

- Plymouth *Encore Worsted* (75% acrylic, 25% wool; 200 yd. [183 m] per 100 g ball), #174 Cranberry (color A), 4 (5, 6, 7) balls, and #1014 Butternut (color B), 1 (1, 2, 2) balls
- Or similar yarn that knits to specified gauge: worsted-weight wool or wool-blend yarn, about 800 (1,000, 1,200, 1,400) yd. [732 (914, 1,097, 1,280) m] of color A and 200 (200, 400, 400) yd. [183 (183, 366, 366) m] of color B
- US 6 [4 mm] needles
- US 7 [4.5 mm] needles
- US 7 [4.5 mm] 16" [40 cm] circular needle
- Stitch marker
- Stitch holders
- Tapestry needle

Gauge

24 sts and 30 rows = 4" [10 cm] over double rib using size 7 [4.5 mm] needles, with rib slightly stretched

QUIDDITCH SWEATER

Designer – Anne Bergeron ☾ Pattern Rating – Ordinary Wizarding Level

Inspired by the house team uniforms in the Harry Potter movies, this sweater knits up quickly in double rib, making it a matter of some simple needle magic to support the house of your choice at the next Quidditch match. Made from a washable wool blend that comes in all the house colors, it should keep you warm and cozy on the pitch all season long, no matter which house you're cheering for!

Front

Using larger needles and color A, CO 94 (106, 118, 130) sts.

Work in double rib, as described in the stitch guide (see page 58), until front measures 11 (11½, 12, 12½)" [28 (29, 30.5, 31.5) cm] or desired length to stripe from CO edge, ending with a WS row completed.

Note: Stripe is worked for 4" before armhole beg on body and sleeves so it will match up when sweater is sewn together. Stretch rib slightly to width measurement before measuring for length.

Change to color B and work 4" [10 cm] in established rib patt, ending with a WS row completed—15 (15½, 16, 16½)" [38 (39, 40.5, 42) cm] or desired length from CO edge. Cut color B, leaving an 8" [20.5 cm] tail.

Begin Armhole Shaping

Maintaining established rib patt, join color A and work decreases as follows:

BO 4 sts beg next 2 rows—86 (98, 110, 122) sts.

BO 0 (2, 2, 3) sts beg next 2 rows—86 (94, 106, 116) sts.

BO 0 (0, 2, 2) sts beg next 2 rows—86 (94, 102, 112) sts.

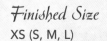

Dec row: Work 1 st in patt, either k2tog or p2tog (using the dec method that maintains the patt), work to last 3 sts, ssk or ssp (using the dec method that maintains the patt), work last st in patt—84 (92, 100, 110) sts.

Rep dec row every other row 3 (5, 7, 8) times more—78 (82, 86, 94) sts.

Work even until armhole measures 4 (4½, 5, 5½)" [11.5 (11.5, 12.5, 14) cm] or desired length from first BO, ending with a WS row completed.

Neck Shaping

Note: Both sides of the front neck are worked at the same time, each with a separate ball of yarn.

Row 1 (RS): Work 36 (36, 37, 40) sts in established patt, drop working yarn and attach a second ball of yarn, work across next 6 (10, 12, 14) sts, place these sts on holder for neck, work rest of row in established patt—36 (36, 37, 40) sts each side of neck.

Row 2 (WS): Work in patt to neck edge, drop yarn, skip sts on holder, pick up first yarn, BO 4 sts, work in patt to end—32 (32, 33, 36) sts rem on side with BO.

Row 3 (RS): Work in patt to neck edge; at other neck edge BO 4 sts, work in patt to end—32 (32, 33, 36) sts each side of neck.

Row 4 (WS): Work in patt to neck edge; at other neck edge BO 2 sts, work in patt to end—30 (30, 31, 34) sts on side with BO.

Row 5 (RS): Work in patt to neck edge; at other neck edge BO 2 sts, work in patt to end—30 (30, 31, 34) sts each side of neck.

Rows 6 and 7: Rep rows 4 and 5 once more—28 (28, 29, 32) sts each side of neck.

Row 8 (WS): Work in patt on both sides of neck.

Row 9 (RS): Work in patt to 3 sts before neck edge, ssk or ssp, work 1 st in patt; at other neck edge work 1 st in patt, k2tog or p2tog, work in patt to end—27 (27, 28, 31) sts each side of neck.

Rep the last 2 rows 6 (6, 6, 7) times more—21 (21, 22, 24) sts each side of neck.

Work even until armholes measure 7 (7½, 8, 8½)" [18 (19, 20.5, 21.5) cm] or desired length from beg of armhole shaping.

Shoulder Shaping

BO 7 (7, 8, 8) sts beg next 2 rows (armhole edge), work in established patt across rem sts—14 (14, 14, 16) sts each side of neck.

Finished Size

XS (S, M, L)

To fit chest: 30 (34, 38, 42)" [76 (86.5, 96.5, 106.5) cm]

Finished chest circumference: 32 (36, 40, 44)" [81.5 (91.5, 101.5, 112) cm], with rib slightly stretched

Note: Ribbing is very elastic and will easily expand 50% or more. However, the more it's stretched, the shorter the piece becomes. To provide the circumference measurements given here, the rib was expanded to provide about 2" [5 cm] ease.

Length: 22¾ (23¾, 24¾, 25¾)" [58 (60.5, 63, 65.5) cm], with rib slightly stretched.

Sample shown: Size M

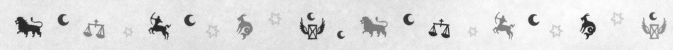

Stitch Guide for This Project

Double Rib (2x2) Worked in Rows over a Multiple of 4 Plus 2 Sts

Row 1: *K2, p2; rep from * to last 2 sts, k2.

Row 2: *P2, k2; rep from * to last 2 sts, p2.

Rep rows 1 and 2.

Single Rib (1x1 Rib) Worked in Rows over an Odd Number of Sts

Row 1: *K1, p1; rep from * to last st, k1.

Row 2: *P1, k1, rep from * to last st, p1.

Rep rows 1 and 2.

Single Rib (1x1 Rib) Worked in Rounds

Rnd 1: *K1, p1; rep from * to end of rnd.

Rep rnd 1.

Special Abbreviations

m1 (Make 1) Purlwise

Insert the left needle tip from front to back under the running strand between the two needles. With right needle, purl into back of strand (twisting the new st to close the hole).

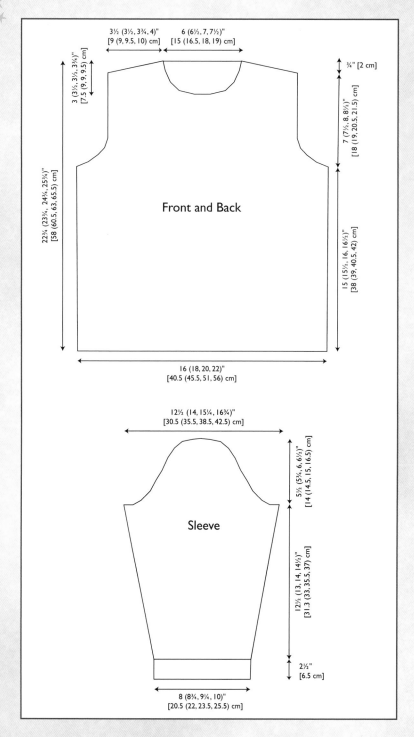

Front and Back

3½ (3½, 3¾, 4)"
[9 (9, 9.5, 10) cm]

6 (6½, 7, 7½)"
[15 (16.5, 18, 19) cm]

3 (3½, 3½, 3¾)"
[7.5 (9, 9, 9.5) cm]

¾" [2 cm]

7 (7½, 8, 8½)"
[18 (19, 20.5, 21.5) cm]

22¾ (23¾, 24¾, 25¾)"
[58 (60.5, 63, 65.5) cm]

15 (15½, 16, 16½)"
[38 (39, 40.5, 42) cm]

16 (18, 20, 22)"
[40.5 (45.5, 51, 56) cm]

Sleeve

12½ (14, 15¼, 16¾)"
[30.5 (35.5, 38.5, 42.5) cm]

5½ (5¾, 6, 6½)"
[14 (14.5, 15, 16.5) cm]

12½ (13, 14, 14½)"
[31.3 (33, 35.5, 37) cm]

2½"
[6.5 cm]

8 (8¾, 9¼, 10)"
[20.5 (22, 23.5, 25.5) cm]

Note: When binding off sts for shoulders, slip the first st of the BO to avoid the "stair step" effect. This leaves a smoother finished line at the shoulder.

BO 7 (7, 7, 8) sts beg next 2 rows (armhole edge), work in established patt across rem sts—7 (7, 7, 8) sts each side of neck.

BO rem sts beg next 2 rows.

Back

Work as for front, including armhole shaping but omitting neck shaping, until work measures 22 (23, 24, 25)" [56 (58.5, 61, 63.5) cm] from CO edge, ending with a WS row completed—78 (82, 86, 94) sts.

Shoulder Shaping

BO 7 (7, 8, 8) sts beg next 2 rows (armhole edge), work in established patt across row—64 (68, 70, 78) sts.

BO 7 (7, 7, 8) sts beg next 2 rows—50 (54, 56, 62) sts.

BO 7 (7, 7, 8) sts beg next 2 rows—36 (40, 42, 46) sts.

BO rem 36 (40, 42, 46) sts.

Sleeves

With smaller needles and color A, CO 53 (57, 61, 65) sts.

Work in single rib in rows, as described in the stitch guide (see page 58), until work measures 2½" [6.5 cm] in length from CO edge, ending with a RS row completed.

Next row (WS): Work in patt to last st, m1 purlwise (see page 58), p1—54 (58, 62, 66) sts.

Change to larger needles and beg working double rib, as described in the stitch guide (see page 58), beg with k2.

Using the backward loop CO method, inc 1 st each end every 5 rows 11 (13, 15, 17) times, working new sts into patt—76 (84, 92, 100) sts. *At the same time,* when sleeve measures about 11 (11½, 12½, 13)" [28 (29, 31.5, 33) cm] or desired length to stripe from CO edge, cut color A, leaving an 8" [20.5 cm] tail, and join color B. Work in color B for 4" [10 cm], ending with a WS row completed.

Note: Sleeve should measure about 15 (15½, 16½, 17)" [38 (39, 42, 43) cm] or desired length from CO edge to top of armhole beg.

Cut color B, leaving an 8" [20.5 cm] tail, and join color A.

Shape Cap

With color A, BO 4 sts beg next 2 rows—68 (76, 84, 92) sts.

BO 0 (2, 2, 3) sts beg next 2 rows—68 (72, 80, 86) sts.

BO 0 (0, 2, 2) sts beg next 2 rows—68 (72, 76, 82) sts.

Dec row (RS): K1, k2tog, work to last 3 sts, ssk, k1—66 (70, 74, 80) sts.

Rep dec row every other row 13 (13, 13, 14) times more—40 (44, 48, 52).

BO 2 sts beg next 8 rows—24 (28, 32, 36) sts.

BO 3 sts beg next 4 rows—12 (16, 20, 24) sts.

BO rem 12 (16, 20, 24) sts.

Join Shoulders

Block each piece, according to yarn manufacturer's instructions.

Backstitch (see page 159) or graft (see page 160) shoulder seams together.

Neckband

Using color B and circ needle, pick up sts around neck edge: With RS facing and beg at left shoulder seam, pick up and k24 (24, 26, 28) sts down left neck edge, place 6 (10, 12, 14) front neck sts back on needle and knit across, pick up and k24 (24, 26, 28) sts along right neck edge, pick up and k36 (40, 42, 46) sts across back neck—90 (98, 106, 116) sts.

Pm at beg of round. Work 3 rnds in single rib, as described in the stitch guide (see page 58). Cut color B, leaving an 8" [20.5 cm] tail.

Join color A and continue in established single rib patt for 22 rnds.

Note: Slip the first st of the second round of color A to make the jump between the rounds less noticeable.

BO loosely in patt.

Fold neckband in half, to WS, and whipstitch (see page 160) in place.

Finishing

Sew side and underarm seams using mattress st (see page 160).

Pin sleeves in place, easing where necessary. With color A threaded on tapestry needle, sew sleeves in place using backstitch (see page 159).

Weave in all rem ends.

Recommended Colors for Other Houses

Slytherin: Plymouth *Encore Worsted* #204 Hunter (color A) and #389 Gray Heather (color B)
Ravenclaw: Plymouth *Encore Worsted* #517 Delft Blue (color A) and #194 Gray Frost (color B)
Hufflepuff: Plymouth *Encore Worsted* #1382 Bright Yellow (color A) and #217 Black (color B)

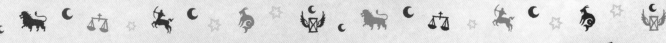

Materials

- Lang *Jawoll Sport* (75% wool, 18% nylon, 7% acrylic; 206 yd. [188 m] per 50 g skein), #8306 Royal Blue (color A), 3 (3, 4) skeins, and #8385 Silver (color B), 1 skein

- Or similar yarn that knits to specified gauge: fingering-weight wool or wool-blend yarn, about 530 (600, 720) yd. [485 (545, 658) m] of color A and about 100 (120, 170) yd. [92 (110, 156) m] of color B, depending on final foot and leg measurements

- US 1 [2.5 mm] double-pointed needles, set of 5

- US 3 [3.25 mm] needle of any type (if using standard BO)

- US 4 [3.5 mm] double-pointed needles (for optional elasticized I-cord BO)

- 1½ yd. [1.37 m] thin elastic cord (for optional elasticized I-cord BO)

- Tapestry needle

Gauge

34 sts and 52 rnds = 4" [10 cm] in St st using size 1 [2.5 mm] needles, without reinforcement thread

QUIDDITCH SOCKS

Designer – Lauren Kent ☾ *Pattern Rating – Ordinary Wizarding Level*

Look your best the next time you head out to the Quidditch pitch with these knee-high striped socks. Knit in durable wool/nylon sock yarn, they'll weather years of abuse in the air and on solid ground without showing the slightest sign of wear, and the optional elastic at the top edge will prevent the dreaded downward creep so common with knee socks. Your legs will be toasty and warm during even the coldest, rainiest matches and comfy as can be under your shin guards. The toe-up construction with a contrasting short-row heel makes it easy to test the fit as you're knitting.

Instructions

Note: Jawoll Sport sock yarn comes as 45 g of wool/acrylic yarn with a 5 g spool of matching nylon reinforcement thread. The thread is shorter than the yarn, so it cannot be used throughout both feet. Depending on foot size, you should have enough thread to use it for both heels and toes, where socks are subject to the most wear, or you can leave it out entirely. If you decide to use the thread, just carry it along with your yarn while knitting. The resulting fabric will be slightly denser and much more durable.

Toe

Using color B and smaller needles, CO 18 (24, 30) sts using the figure-eight cast-on method (see page 155).

Work in St st for 2 rnds, then divide sts onto four dpns, keeping half the total number of sts on the first two needles and the other half on the 3rd and 4th needles.

Rnd 1 (inc rnd): *K2, k1b into previous st, k5 (8, 11), k1b into next st, k2; rep from * to end of rnd—22 (28, 34) sts.

Rnd 2: Knit.

Rnd 3 (inc rnd): *K2, k1b into previous st, knit to 2 sts before end of needle 2, k1b into next st, k2; rep from * to end of rnd—26 (32, 38) sts.

Rnd 4: Knit.

Rep rnds 3 and 4 until you have worked a total of 12 inc rnds— 66 (72, 78) sts. Tighten the original sts from your CO.

Foot

Work 3 rnds in St st.

Rnd 1: K16 (18, 20), cut color B and join color A, k50 (54, 58).

Rnd 2: K32 (38, 38), [p2, k4] 5 (5, 6) times, p2, k2.

Continuing with color A, rep rnd 2 until the sock measures 1⅞ (2, 2⅛)" [4.7 (5, 5.3) cm] shorter than total foot length.

Heel

Note: The heel is shaped using short rows, worked back and forth across the sole—over the sts that have been worked in St st thus far. The other half of the sts (those that have been ribbed) can be left on their needles or slipped onto scrap yarn for safekeeping. For instructions on how to wrap sts, yback, and yfwd, see *Special Techniques for This Project,* page 64.

Setup row (WS): With inside of St st sole facing you, join color B at the end of needle 2, p33 (36, 39). Do not cut color A.

Decrease the Heel

Row 1 (RS): K32 (35, 38), wrap next st, turn work.

Row 2 (WS): P31 (34, 37), wrap next st, turn work, yback (between 1st and 2nd sts).

Row 3: K30 (33, 36), wrap next st, turn work.

Row 4: P29 (32, 35), wrap next st, turn work, yback (between 2nd and 3rd sts).

Row 5: K28 (31, 34), wrap next st, turn work.

Finished Size

S (M, L)

Circumference at ball of foot (unstretched): 6¾ (7½, 8¼)" [17 (19, 21) cm]

Circumference at calf (unstretched): 6 (8, 8)" [15 (20.5, 20.5) cm]

Foot length: Customizable

Leg length: Customizable

Sample shown: Size M

Note: Whenever possible, length measurements should be made with the sock tried on. The ribbed fabric will stretch to 150%–200% of its relaxed width, decreasing the sock's length in the process. For this reason, many length measurements are provided in inches/ centimeters rather than rows.

Stitch Guide for This Project

Stockinette Stitch (St st) Worked in Rounds

Knit all sts.

4x2 Rib Worked in Rounds (Multiple of 6 Sts)

Rnd 1: *P2, k4; rep from * to end of rnd.

Rep rnd 1.

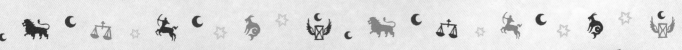

Special Techniques for This Project

k1b (Lifted Increase) into Previous Stitch

With the previous st on the right needle, insert the left needle into the purl bump 2 rows below the st on the needle and knit the st.

k1b (Lifted Increase) into Next Stitch

Roll the left needle forward, toward you, exposing the purl sts. Insert the right needle tip from top to bottom into the first purl bump on the left needle and knit; the active st (still on the left needle) is counted as the next st in the following instructions.

yback (Yarn Back)

Bring yarn back between needles (as if to knit).

yfwd (Yarn Forward)

Bring yarn forward between needles (as if to purl).

Wrap Next St (RS)

Yfwd, sl next st pwise to right needle, yback, sl that st pwise back to left needle.

Wrap Next St (WS)

Sl next st pwise to right needle, yback, sl that st pwise back to left needle.

Knit Next Wrapped St

Using right needle, pick up both loops of yarn wrapped at base of next st and place them on the left needle, then k3tog.

Purl Next Wrapped St

Using right needle, pick up both loops of yarn wrapped at base of next st and place them on left needle, then p3tog.

Row 6: P27 (30, 33), wrap next st, turn work, yback (between 3rd and 4th sts).

Row 7: K26 (29, 32), wrap next st, turn work.

Row 8: P25 (28, 31), wrap next st, turn work, yback (between 4th and 5th sts).

Row 9: K24 (27, 30), wrap next st, turn work.

Row 10: P23 (26, 29), wrap next st, turn work, yback (between 5th and 6th sts).

Row 11: K22 (25, 28), wrap next st, turn work.

Row 12: P21 (24, 27), wrap next st, turn work, yback (between 6th and 7th sts).

Row 13: K20 (23, 26), wrap next st, turn work.

Row 14: P19 (22, 25), wrap next st, turn work, yback (between 7th and 8th sts).

Row 15: K18 (21, 24), wrap next st, turn work.

Row 16: P17 (20, 23), wrap next st, turn work, yback (between 8th and 9th sts).

Row 17: K16 (19, 22), wrap next st, turn work.

Row 18: P15 (18, 21), wrap next st, turn work, yback (between 9th and 10th sts).

Row 19: K14 (17, 20), wrap next st, turn work.

Row 20: P13 (16, 19), wrap next st, turn work, yback (between 10th and 11th sts).

For size S, go to *All Sizes: Widen the Heel*. For sizes M and L, continue short rows as follows.

Sizes M and L Only

Row 21: K– (15, 18), wrap next st, turn work.

Row 22: P– (14, 17), wrap next st, turn work, yback (between 11th and 12th sts).

Row 23: K– (13, 16), wrap next st, turn work.

Row 24: P– (12, 15), wrap next st, turn work, yback (between 12th and 13th sts).

For size M, go to *All Sizes: Widen the Heel*. For size L, continue short rows as follows.

Row 25: K– (–, 14), wrap next st, turn work.

Row 26: P– (–, 13), wrap next st, turn work, yback (between 13th and 14th sts).

Row 27: K– (–, 12), wrap next st, turn work.

Row 28: P– (–, 11), wrap next st, turn work, yback (between 14th and 15th sts).

All Sizes: Widen the Heel

Note: Widening the heel involves knitting and purling wrapped stitches as described in *Special Techniques for This Project* (see page 64).

Next row: K13 (12, 11), wrap next st again, turn work.

Next row: P13 (12, 11), wrap next st again, turn work, yback.

Work short rows as follows:

Row 1 (RS): K13 (12, 11), knit next wrapped st, wrap next st, turn work.

Row 2 (WS): P14 (13, 12), purl next wrapped st, wrap next st, turn work, yback.

Row 3: K15 (14, 13), knit next wrapped st, wrap next st, turn work.

Row 4: P16 (15, 14), purl next wrapped st, wrap next st, turn work, yback.

Row 5: K17 (16, 15), knit next wrapped st, wrap next st, turn work.

Row 6: P18 (17, 16), purl next wrapped st, wrap next st, turn work, yback.

Row 7: K19 (18, 17), knit next wrapped st, wrap next st, turn work.

Row 8: P20 (19, 18), purl next wrapped st, wrap next st, turn work, yback.

Row 9: K21 (20, 19), knit next wrapped st, wrap next st, turn work.

Row 10: P22 (21, 20), purl next wrapped st, wrap next st, turn work, yback.

Row 11: K23 (22, 21), knit next wrapped st, wrap next st, turn work.

Row 12: P24 (23, 22), purl next wrapped st, wrap next st, turn work, yback.

Row 13: K25 (24, 23), knit next wrapped st, wrap next st, turn work.

Row 14: P26 (25, 24), purl next wrapped st, wrap next st, turn work, yback.

Row 15: K27 (26, 25), knit next wrapped st, wrap next st, turn work.

Row 16: P28 (27, 26), purl next wrapped st, wrap next st, turn work, yback.

Row 17: K29 (28, 27), knit next wrapped st, wrap next st, turn work.

Row 18: P30 (29, 28), purl next wrapped st, wrap next st, turn work, yback.

For size S, go to *All Sizes: Finish Heel.* For sizes M and L, continue short rows as follows.

Sizes M and L Only

Row 19: K– (30, 29), knit next wrapped st, wrap next st, turn work.

Row 20: P– (31, 30), purl next wrapped st, wrap next st, turn work, yback.

Row 21: K– (32, 31), knit next wrapped st, wrap next st, turn work.

Row 22: P– (33, 32), purl next wrapped st, wrap next st, turn work, yback.

For size M, go to *All Sizes: Finish Heel*. For size L, continue short rows as follows.

Size L Only

Row 23: K– (–, 33), knit next wrapped st, wrap next st, turn work.

Row 24: P– (–, 34), purl next wrapped st, wrap next st, turn work, yback.

Row 25: K– (–, 35), knit next wrapped st, wrap next st, turn work.

Row 26: P– (–, 36), purl next wrapped st, wrap next st, turn work, yback.

All Sizes: Finish Heel

Next row: K31 (34, 37), knit next wrapped st, turn work.

Next row: P32 (35, 38), purl next wrapped st, turn work.

Return instep sts to needles, if necessary, and return to circular knitting.

Next rnd: Cut color B, pick up color A and k33 (36, 39) heel sts, p1 (0, 1), k4 (2, 4), [p2, k4] 4 (5, 5) times, p2, k2.

Leg

Rnd 1: K2, [p2, k4] 10 (11, 12) times, p2, k2.

Rep 4x2 rib as in rnd 1 until you reach the base of the calf muscle, usually about halfway up the lower leg.

Begin increases for calf:

Rnd 1: K2, [p2, k4] 2 times, p2, k2, m1, k2, [p2, k4] 7 (8, 9) times, p2, k2—67 (73, 79) sts.

Rnd 2: K2, [p2, k4] 2 times, p2, k5, [p2, k4] 7 (8, 9) times, p2, k2.

Rnd 3: K2, [p2, k4] 2 times, p2, k3, m1, k2, [p2, k4] 7 (8, 9) times, p2, k2—68 (74, 80) sts.

Rnd 4: K2, [p2, k4] 2 times, p2, k6, [p2, k4] 7 (8, 9) times, p2, k2.

Rnd 5: K2, [p2, k4] 2 times, p2, k3, m1, k3, [p2, k4] 7 (8, 9) times, p2, k2—69 (75, 81) sts.

Rnd 6: K2, [p2, k4] 2 times, p2, k3, p1, k3, [p2, k4] 7 (8, 9) times, p2, k2.

Rnd 7: K2, [p2, k4] 2 times, p2, k3, p1, m1, k3, [p2, k4] 7 (8, 9) times, p2, k2—70 (76, 82) sts.

Rnd 8: K2, [p2, k4] 2 times, p2, k3, p2, k3, [p2, k4] 7 (8, 9) times, p2, k2.

Rnd 9: K2, [p2, k4] 2 times, p2, k2, m1, k1, p2, k1, m1, k2, [p2, k4] 7 (8, 9) times, p2, k2—72 (78, 84) sts.

Rnd 10: K2, [p2, k4] 11 (12, 13) times, p2, k2.

Work even in 4x2 rib for 1¼" [3 cm].

For narrow calves, work even for another 10 rnds; pick up directions at Rnd 11, below. For average and muscular calves, inc as follows:

Rnd 1: K2, [p2, k4] 2 times, [p2, k2, m1, k2] 2 times, [p2, k4] 7 (8, 9) times, p2, k2—74 (80, 86) sts.

Rnd 2: K2, [p2, k4] 2 times, [p2, k5] 2 times, [p2, k4] 7 (8, 9) times, p2, k2.

Rnd 3: K2, [p2, k4] 2 times, [p2, k3, m1, k2] 2 times, [p2, k4] 7 (8, 9) times, p2, k2—76 (82, 88) sts.

Rnd 4: K2, [p2, k4] 2 times, [p2, k6] 2 times, [p2, k4] 7 (8, 9) times, p2, k2.

Rnd 5: K2, [p2, k4] 2 times, [p2, k3, m1, k3] 2 times, [p2, k4] 7 (8, 9) times, p2, k2—78 (84, 90) sts.

Rnd 6: K2, [p2, k4] 2 times, [p2, k3, p1, k3] 2 times, [p2, k4] 7 (8, 9) times, p2, k2.

Rnd 7: K2, [p2, k4] 2 times, [p2, k3, p1, m1, k3] 2 times, [p2, k4] 7 (8, 9) times, p2, k2—80 (86, 92) sts.

Rnd 8: K2, [p2, k4] 2 times, [p2, k3, p2, k3] 2 times, [p2, k4] 7 (8, 9) times, p2, k2.

Rnd 9: K2, [p2, k4] 2 times, [p2, k2, m1, k1, p2, k1, m1, k2] 2 times, [p2, k4] 7 (8, 9) times, p2, k2—84 (90, 96) sts.

Rnd 10: K2, [p2, k4] 13 (14, 15) times, p2, k2.

Rnd 11: Join color B and knit all sts.

Note: At this point, you can either cut color A or leave it attached and catch it between sts in front of the working yarn every 2–3 rnds.

Work even in 4x2 rib patt with color B for 1¼" [3 cm].

Next rnd: Change to color A and knit all sts.

Work even in 4x2 rib patt with color A for 2½" [6.5 cm].

Next rnd: Change to color B and knit all sts.

Work even in 4x2 rib patt with color B for 1¼" [3 cm].

Next rnd: Change to color A and knit all sts. Cut color B.

Work even in 4x2 rib patt with color A for 1½" [4 cm].

BO very loosely, using larger needle, or use elasticized I-cord bind-off, as follows.

Elasticized I-Cord Bind-off (Optional)

To create an elastic top edge to prevent the socks from sneaking down, you can use this bind-off method instead of the standard BO. Cut yarn and join it at the *left needle* by threading it through the first st and knotting the yarn. CO 3 sts.

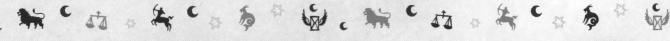

Using a larger dpn, k2, k2tog (with 1 newly cast-on st and 1 old st). *Slide these 3 sts to the other end of the dpn and, using the other dpn, k2, sl last st to smaller needle, k2tog.* Rep from * to * until all sts have been bound off and 3 sts remain on the dpn. Sl the first 2 sts over the most recent st (to which the yarn is attached), then cut yarn and knot it through the most recent st, leaving an 8" [20.5 cm] tail.

Using a tapestry needle and starting at the back of the sock, thread elastic cord through the small tubular casing formed by the I-cord bind-off. Knot ends of elastic together so that top of sock fits snugly but not too tightly. Lace the yarn tail from the BO back and forth over the knot to conceal it.

Finishing

If necessary, tighten the CO sts at the toe.

Weave in all rem ends.

Block, if desired, according to yarn manufacturer's instructions.

Recommended Colors for Other Houses

Gryffindor: Lang *Jawoll Sport* #8361 Beet (color A) and #8343 Yellow (color B)

Slytherin: Lang *Jawoll Sport* #83117 Green (color A) and #8385 Silver (color B)

Ravenclaw: Lang *Jawoll Sport* #8306 Royal Blue (color A) and #83139 Warm Brown (color B)

Hufflepuff: Lang *Jawoll Sport* #8343 Yellow (color A) and #8304 Black (color B)

House Colors

Gryffindor, Ravenclaw, Hufflepuff, or Slytherin? Once the Sorting Hat has placed you, you need the proper uniform. These patterns will help you dress the part right. Here you'll find the ever-popular house scarf, along with matching hats, mittens, and socks. Of course, no uniform would be complete without the traditional v-neck house sweater. And while fashion-minded kids can knit themselves funky hip scarves, the more studious can whip up mini-scarves to use as bookmarks.

The signature striped scarves seen in the movies provide the stripe styles seen on most of the items in this section. And like the scarves, most of the other knits are worked in worsted-weight wool or wool blends, so you can choose one yarn you like best and use the patterns to knit an entire matching set. Recommendations are provided for color choices for all the houses, so no matter who you're rooting for on the Quidditch pitch, you can be dressed in your house colors from head to toe!

Materials for Year 1-2 Scarf

- ☾ Cascade Yarns *220* (100% wool; 220 yd. [201 m] per 100 g ball), #2413 Burgundy (color A), 2 (3) skeins, and #7827 Gold (color B), 2 skeins
- ☾ Or similar yarn that knits to specified gauge: worsted-weight wool or wool-blend yarn, about 315 (460) yd. [288 (420) m] of color A and 282 (440) yd. [258 (402) m] of color B
- ☾ US 8 [5 mm] 16" [40 cm] circular needle
- ☾ Stitch marker
- ☾ US J [6 mm] crochet hook
- ☾ Tapestry needle

Gauge

20 sts and 26 rnds = 4" [10 cm] in St st using size 8 [5 mm] needles

Finished Size

S (L)

Width: 5½ (7)" [14 (18) cm]

Length: 55½ (70)" [141 (178) cm], without fringe

Sample shown: Size L

HOUSE SCARVES

Designer – Lauren Kent ☾ *Pattern Rating – First Year*

When it comes to Harry Potter knits, these scarves are the standard. Offered in two styles—a wide stripe, stockinette stitch tube scarf based on the ones worn by Hogwarts students in the first two movies and a narrow stripe design, worked in rib, based on the scarves worn in the third and fourth movies—their look is signature Harry Potter. Cascade Yarns *220* is a great yarn for this project because it has wonderful stitch definition, is very economical, and comes in all the house colors!

Year 1–2 Scarf

This scarf has been the starting point for countless fans-turned-knitters over the years. How better to show your (or a friend's) house loyalty and fannish pride than with the original scarf? Nineteen bold regimental stripes grace this double-thickness scarf in a great first project—and because it's knit as a tube in the round, you don't even need to purl. If you're concerned with the washability of the scarf, try a wool/acrylic blend such as Plymouth *Encore Worsted*.

Instructions

With color A, CO 55 (70) sts, place marker to note beg rnd, and join in a circle, being careful not to twist sts.

Work in St st as described in the stitch guide, changing colors as described in the stripe pattern.

Complete 19 alternating stripes, ending with color A. BO all sts. Cut yarn, leaving an 8" [20.5 cm] tail.

Finishing

Weave in CO and BO tails only. Trim tails from color changes to 1½" [4 cm] long; they can be left loose on the inside of the scarf, as they won't be seen.

Block scarf, if desired, according to yarn manufacturer's instructions.

Add Fringe

There should be 11 fringe groups at each end of the scarf, 6 in color A and 5 in color B, alternating.

Cut 60 (84) pieces of color A and 50 (70) pieces of color B, each 15" [38 cm] long. (Or cut a piece of cardboard that is 7½" [19 cm] wide and wind the yarn around it. Then cut the yarn wraps at one edge.)

To make each fringe group, hold 5 (7) pieces of yarn together and fold them in half. Push crochet hook through both layers of knitting; catch the folded loops of yarn, and pull them through the knitting. With loop still on crochet hook, catch long ends of yarn and pull through loop to secure. Remove the hook, thread the cut yarn ends through the loops, and tighten the fringe.

Space the fringe groups evenly across the ends of the scarf, beginning and ending with color A.

When all the fringe has been tied, trim yarn ends to a uniform length.

Stitch Guide for This Project

Stockinette Stitch (St st)
Worked in Rounds
Knit all sts.

Stripe Pattern

Work 18 (23) rnds color A, *19 (24) rnds color B, 19 (24) rnds color A; rep from * to end of scarf.

Note: At color changes, break old color and join new one with 8" [20.5 cm] tails and work for 2 rnds. Then go back to join point, tighten sts as necessary, and tie tails using an overhand knot.

Materials for Year 3–4 Scarf

- ☾ Cascade Yarns *220* (100% wool; 220 yd. [201 m] per 100 g ball): #9404 Wine (color A), 3 (4) skeins, and #7827 Gold (color B), 1 skein
- ☾ Or similar yarn that knits to specified gauge: worsted-weight wool or wool-blend yarn, about 525 (860) yd. [480 (786) m] of color A and 70 (90) yd. [64 (82) m] of color B
- ☾ US 6 [4 mm] needles
- ☾ Stitch marker
- ☾ US G [4 mm] crochet hook
- ☾ Tapestry needle

Gauge

32 sts and 28 rows = 4" [10 cm] in single rib (in relaxed state) using size 6 [4 mm] needles

Finished Size

S (L)

Width: 7 (9)" [18 (23) cm]

Length: 58¾ (80)" [149 (203) cm], without fringe

Sample shown: Size S

Year 3–4 Scarf

If you're looking for a scarf that's a bit more incognito than the Year 1–2 scarf, this is the one for you. Introduced with the revamped uniforms of the third movie, this trapped bar scarf lets true fans know your house, while Muggles remain unaware. In place of the stockinette-tube construction of the first scarf, this is knit flat in single rib, which pulls in on itself to produce an equally cozy fabric. This new scarf is larger than its predecessor, so adults may want to consider the smaller size unless they want a film-accurate piece.

Instructions

With color A, CO 57 (73) sts.

Work in single rib, as described in the stitch guide, on all rows, changing colors as described in the stripe pattern.

Work until the scarf has 14 pairs of color B bars and 15 larger color A stripes, ending with color A. BO all sts. Cut yarn, leaving an 8" [20.5 cm] tail.

Finishing

Weave in tails on WS of scarf.

Block scarf, if desired, according to yarn manufacturer's instructions.

Add Fringe

Cut 112 (144) pieces of color A, each 6" [15 cm] long. (Or cut a piece of cardboard that is 3" [7.5 cm] wide and wind the yarn around it. Then cut the yarn wraps at one edge.)

To make each fringe group, hold 2 pieces of yarn together and fold them in half. With RS facing you, push crochet hook through the scarf, just above the CO/BO edge, at the left-most column of purl sts; catch the folded loops of yarn and pull them through the knitting. Remove the hook, thread the cut yarn ends through the loops, and tighten the fringe. Rep at each purl "valley" across each end of the scarf.

When all the fringe has been tied, trim yarn ends to a length of about 1½" [4 cm].

Stitch Guide for This Project

Single Rib (1x1 Rib) Worked in Rows

Row 1 (WS): Sl 1 pwise, *p1, k1; rep from * to end of row.

Row 2 (RS): Sl 1 pwise, *k1, p1; rep from * to end of row.

Rep rows 1 and 2 for patt, except for the first 2 rows after any color change. Work those 2 rows as follows:

Row 1 (WS): K1, *p1, k1; rep from * to end of row.

Row 2 (RS): P1, *k1, p1; rep from * to end of row.

Working the 2 rows after each color change this way prevents the selvedge sts from mismatching the rest of the row.

Stripe Pattern

Work 19 (29) rows color A, *2 rows color B, 4 rows color A, 2 rows color B, 20 (30) rows color A; rep from * to end of scarf.

Note: To reduce the number of ends to weave in, carry the non-working color up the side while working the shorter stripes by catching it between stitches.

Recommended Colors for Other Houses

Slytherin: Cascade Yarns *220* #8893 Forest Green (color A) and #8401 Light Gray (color B)

Ravenclaw: Cascade Yarns *220* #8886 Navy (color A) and #8401 Light Gray (color B) or #8886 Navy (color A) and #2415 Bronze (color B)

Hufflepuff: Cascade Yarns *220* #7827 Gold (color A) and #8555 Black (color B)

Materials

- ☽ Plymouth *Encore Worsted* (75% acrylic, 25% wool; 200 yd. [183 m] per 100 g ball), #999 Burnt Sienna (color A), 1 skein, and #1014 Butternut (color B), 1 skein

- ☽ Or similar yarn that knits to specified gauge: worsted-weight wool or wool-blend yarn. The following amounts are based on the largest size:

  Beanie, Wide Stripes version: about 65 yd. [60 m] each of color A and color B

  Beanie, Narrow Stripes version: about 115 yd. [105 m] of color A and 15 yd. [14 m] of color B

  Beret, Wide Stripes version: about 80 yd. [73 m] of color A and 70 yd. [64 m] of color B

  Beret, Narrow Stripes version: about 145 yd. [132 m] of color A and 20 yd. [18 m] of color B

- ☽ US 6 [4 mm] 16" [40 cm] circular needle

- ☽ US 7 [4.5 mm] 16" [40 cm] circular needle

- ☽ US 7 [4.5 mm] double-pointed needles

- ☽ Stitch markers

- ☽ Tapestry needle

Gauge

18 sts and 26 rnds = 4" [10 cm] in St st using size 7 [4.5 mm] needles

HOUSE HATS

Designer – Alison Hansel ☽ *Pattern Rating – First Year*

A boy's beanie and a girl's beret to show off your school colors! They may not be magic, but these easy-to-knit hats will keep you warm and in style at the same time. The beanie has paired decreases at the crown for a more masculine and contemporary look, and the beret offers a feminine alternative to the standard hat shape. They're both knit in a practical and machine-washable acrylic/wool yarn that comes in all the Hogwarts house colors, so you can pick your house and your stripes and have house-head all winter long!

Beanie

Instructions

With smaller needles and color A, CO 84 (96, 108) sts, pm to note beg rnd, and join in a circle, being careful not to twist sts.

Edging

Work in single rib, as described in the stitch guide, for 6 rnds.

Body

Change to larger needles and work desired stripe patt in St st, beg with color B for Wide Stripes pattern and continuing with color A for Narrow Stripes pattern. Work in this manner until hat measures 5 (5½, 6)" [12.5 (14, 15) cm] from CO edge.

Next rnd: *K21 (24, 27); pm, rep from * to end of rnd—4 markers in place.

Decrease for Top

Change to dpns when too few sts remain to continue on circ needle.

Rnd 1: *K2tog, k17 (20, 23), ssk; rep from * to end of rnd—76 (88, 100) sts.

Rnds 2, 4, 6, 8, and 10: Knit.

Rnd 3: *K2tog, k15 (18, 21), ssk; rep from * to end of rnd—68 (80, 92) sts.

Rnd 5: *K2tog, k13 (16, 19), ssk; rep from * to end of rnd—60 (72, 84) sts.

Rnd 7: *K2tog, k11 (14, 17), ssk; rep from * to end of rnd—52 (64, 76) sts.

Rnd 9: *K2tog, k9 (12, 15), ssk; rep from * to end of rnd—44 (56, 68) sts.

Rnd 11: *K2tog, k7 (10, 13), ssk; rep from * to end of rnd—36 (48, 60) sts.

Rnd 12: *K2tog, k5 (8, 11), ssk; rep from * to end of rnd—28 (40, 52) sts.

Rnd 13: *K2tog, k3 (6, 9), ssk; rep from * to end of rnd—20 (32, 44) sts.

Rnd 14: *K2tog, k1 (4, 7), ssk; rep from * to end of rnd—12 (24, 36) sts.

Finished Size

S (M, L)

Circumference: 18½ (21¼, 24)" [47 (54, 61) cm]

Length: Beanie, 7½ (8, 8½)" [19 (20.5, 21.5) cm], and Beret, 7 (7½, 8)" [18 (19, 20.5) cm]

Samples shown: Beret, size S, and Beanie, size M

Stitch Guide for This Project

Single Rib (1x1 Rib) Worked in Rounds

Rnd 1: *K1, p1; rep from * to end of rnd.

Rep rnd 1.

Stockinette Stitch (St st) Worked in Rounds

Knit all sts.

Stripe Patterns

Wide Stripes

Work 6 rnds color A, 6 rnds color B; rep from * for remainder of hat, adjusting the number of rnds worked in the final stripe according to hat instructions.

Narrow Stripes

Work with color A until hat measures 3 (3½, 4)" [7.5 (9, 10) cm] from CO edge. Then work 2 rnds color B, 3 rnds color A, 2 rnds color B, and return to color A for remainder of hat.

Note: Carry yarn not in use loosely across the skipped rnds.

Sizes M and L Only

Continue decreases for sizes M and L only:

> **Rnd 15:** *K2tog, k– (2, 5), ssk; rep from * to end of rnd—12 (16, 28) sts.
>
> **Rnd 16:** *K2tog, k– (0, 3), ssk; rep from * to end of rnd—12 (8, 20) sts.

Size L Only

Continue decreases for size L only:

> **Rnd 17:** *K2tog, k– (–, 1), ssk; rep from * to end of rnd—12 (8, 12) sts.

Finishing

Cut yarn, leaving an 8" [20.5 cm] tail, and thread tail through rem 12 (8, 12) sts to close top of hat.

Weave in ends.

Block beanie, if desired, according to yarn manufacturer's instructions.

Beret

Instructions

With smaller needles and color A, CO 84 (96, 108) sts, pm to note beg rnd, and join in a circle, being careful not to twist sts.

Edging

Work in single rib, as described in the stitch guide (see page 75), for 6 rnds.

Increase for Body

Switching to larger needles and working desired stripe pattern (beg with color B for Wide Stripes pattern and continuing with color A for Narrow Stripes pattern), work increases:

> **Rnd 1:** *K5, k1f&b; rep from * to end of rnd—98 (112, 126) sts.
>
> **Rnd 2:** Knit.
>
> **Rnd 3:** *K6, k1f&b; rep from * to end of rnd—112 (128, 144) sts.

Work even (without further increases) in St st until hat measures 5½ (6, 6½)" [14 (15, 16.5) cm] from CO edge.

Decrease for Top

Change to dpns when too few sts remain to continue on circ needle.

Rnd 1: *K6, k2tog; rep from * to end of rnd—98 (112, 126) sts.

Rnds 2, 4, 6, and 8: Knit.

Rnd 3: *K5, k2tog; rep from * to end of rnd—84 (96, 108) sts.

Rnd 5: *K4, k2tog; rep from * to end of rnd—70 (80, 90) sts.

Rnd 7: *K3, k2tog; rep from * to end of rnd—56 (64, 72) sts.

Rnd 9: *K2, k2tog; rep from * to end of rnd—42 (48, 54) sts.

Rnd 10: *K1, k2tog; rep from * to end of rnd—28 (32, 36) sts.

Rnd 11: *K2tog; rep from * to end of rnd—14 (16, 18) sts.

Rnd 12: Rep rnd 11—7 (8, 9) sts.

Finishing

Cut yarn, leaving an 8" [20.5 cm] tail, and thread tail through rem stitches to close top of hat.

Weave in ends.

Block beret, if desired, according to yarn manufacturer's instructions.

Recommended Colors for Other Houses

Slytherin: Plymouth *Encore Worsted* #204 Hunter (color A) and #389 Gray Heather (color B)

Ravenclaw: Plymouth *Encore Worsted* #517 Delft Blue (color A) and #194 Gray Frost (color B)

Hufflepuff: Plymouth *Encore Worsted* #217 Black (color A) and #1382 Bright Yellow (color B)

Materials

- Cascade *220 Superwash* (100% superwash wool, 220 yd. [201 m] per 100 g ball):

  Narrow Stripes version: #855 Maroon (color A), 1 skein, and #821 Marigold (color B), 1 skein

  Wide Stripes version: #801 Army Green (color A), 1 skein, and #816 Gray (color B), 1 skein

- Or similar yarn that knits to specified gauge: worsted-weight wool or wool-blend yarn:

  Narrow Stripes version: About 100 (140, 180) yd. [91.5 (128, 164.5) m] of color A and 4 yd. [3.5 m] of color B

  Wide Stripes version: About 50 (70, 90) yd. [45.7 (64, 82) m] each of colors A and B

- US 5 [3.75 mm] double-pointed needles, set of 5
- Stitch markers
- Tapestry needle

Gauge

23 sts and 32 rnds = 4" [10 cm] in St st using size 5 [3.75 mm] needles

Finished Size

S (M, L)

Hand circumference: 5½ (7, 8¼)" [14 (18, 21) cm]

Length: 8 (10, 11)" [20.5 (25.5, 28) cm]

Samples shown: Size M

HOUSE MITTENS

Designer – Alison Hansel ☾ *Pattern Rating – First Year*

House stripes for your hands! Mittens are a great intro project for knitting in the round. And the classic stripes look awesome on a mitten. The yarn used here is 100% super-wash wool that comes in all the Harry Potter colors and more. Knitting the worsted-weight yarn on US 5 [3.75 mm] needles makes these mittens nice and cozy to keep those hands warm at Quidditch matches this fall!

Right Mitten

With color A, CO 32 (40, 48) sts, distribute stitches so that there are 8 (10, 12) sts on each of four dpns, and join in a circle, being careful not to twist sts.

Cuff

Work in single rib, as described in the stitch guide, following desired stripe pattern, for 1½ (2, 2½)" [4 (5, 6.5) cm].

Continuing in desired stripe pattern, work 2 rnds St st.

Increase for Thumb Gusset

Rnd 1: Needles 1 and 2: knit all sts; needle 3: k7 (9, 11), pm, k1f&b; needle 4: k1f&b, pm, k7 (9, 11)—34 (42, 50) sts.

Rnds 2, 3, 5, and 6: Knit.

Rnd 4: Needles 1 and 2: knit all sts; needle 3: k7 (9, 11), slip marker, k1f&b, k1; needle 4: k1, k1f&b, slip marker, k7 (9, 11)—36 (44, 52) sts.

Rnd 7: Needles 1 and 2: knit all sts; needle 3: k7 (9, 11), slip marker, k1f&b, k2; needle 4: k2, k1f&b, slip marker, k7 (9, 11)—38 (46, 54) sts.

Continue in this manner, increasing on needle 3 and needle 4 every third row, until 6 (7, 8) increases have been completed and there are 14 (16, 18) thumb sts between markers—44 (54, 64) sts.

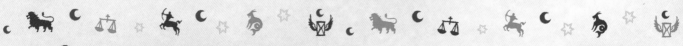

Next rnd: Knit to first marker, remove marker, k1, slip rem 13 (15, 17) thumb sts onto a scrap of yarn, remove second marker, knit to end of rnd.

Next rnd: Knit to thumb gap. Using the backward loop method, CO 1 stitch and join to continue in the round with stitches on other side of thumb—32 (40, 48) sts.

Work until mitten measures approximately 7 (8, 8¼)" [18 (20.5, 21) cm] from CO edge, then begin hand decreases as follows, according to size.

Decrease the Hand

Size S Only

Decrease as follows for size S:

Rnd 1: *K6, k2tog; rep from * to end of rnd—28 sts.
Rnd 2: *K5, k2tog; rep from * to end of rnd—24 sts.
Rnd 3: *K4, k2tog; rep from * to end of rnd—20 sts.
Rnd 4: *K3, k2tog; rep from * to end of rnd—16 sts.
Rnd 5: *K2, k2tog; rep from * to end of rnd—12 sts.

Stitch Guide for This Project

Single Rib (1x1 Rib) Worked in Rounds

Rnd 1: *K1, p1; rep from * to end of rnd.

Rep rnd 1.

Stockinette Stitch (St st) Worked in Rounds

Knit all sts.

Stripe Patterns

Wide Stripes

*Work 8 rnds color A, 8 rnds color B; rep from * for remainder of mitten, adjusting the number of rnds worked in the final stripe according to instructions.

Narrow Stripes

Work with color A until 3 (5, 5) rnds have been knitted after the thumb gusset is complete. Then work 2 rnds color B, 3 rnds color A, 2 rnds color B, and return to color A for remainder of mitten.

Note: Carry yarn not in use loosely upward at the beginning of each of the skipped rnds.

Rnd 6: *K1, k2tog; rep from * to end of rnd—8 sts.

Rnd 7: *K2tog; rep from * to end of rnd—4 sts.

Size M Only

Decrease as follows for size M:

Rnd 1: *K8, k2tog; rep from * to end of rnd—36 sts.

Rnds 2 and 4: Knit.

Rnd 3: *K7, k2tog; rep from * to end of rnd—32 sts.

Rnds 5–11: Work same as size S rnds 1–7 until 4 sts rem.

Size L Only

Decrease as follows for size L only:

Rnd 1: *K10, k2tog; rep from * to end of rnd—44 sts.

Rnds 2 and 4: Knit.

Rnd 3: *K9, k2tog; rep from * to end of rnd—40 sts.

Rnds 5–8: Work same as size M rnds 1–4 until 32 sts rem.

Rnds 9–15: Work same as size S rnds 1–7 until 4 sts rem.

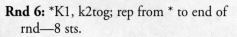

Close Top: All Sizes

Cut yarn, leaving an 8" [20.5 cm] tail, and thread tail through rem 4 sts to close top of mitten.

Work Thumb

Place 13 (15, 17) thumb sts on three dpns. Rejoin yarn at palm side of thumb and knit across all needles. With third dpn, pick up 3 sts from hand section of mitten over gap—16 (18, 20) sts.

Work in St st in the round for 1 (1½, 1¾)" [2.5 (4, 4.5) cm] or to middle of thumbnail.

Decrease Thumb

Rnd 1: *K2 (1, 3), k2tog; rep from * to end of rnd—12 (12, 16) sts.

Rnd 2: *K2tog; rep from * to end of rnd—6 (6, 8) sts.

Rnd 3: Rep rnd 2—3 (3, 4) sts.

Close Thumb: All Sizes

Cut yarn, leaving an 8" [20.5 cm] tail, and thread tail through rem 3 (3, 4) sts to close top of thumb.

Left Mitten

Work as for Right Mitten to *Increase for Thumb Gusset* (see page 78). Then increase as follows.

Increase for Thumb Gusset

Rnd 1: Needle 1: k7 (9, 11), pm, k1f&b; needle 2: k1f&b, pm, k7 (9, 11); needles 3 and 4: knit— 34 (42, 50) sts.

Rnds 2, 3, 5, and 6: Knit.

Rnd 4: Needle 1: k7 (9, 11), slip marker, k1f&b, k1; needle 2: k1, k1f&b, slip marker, k7 (9, 11); needles 3 and 4: knit—36 (44, 52) sts.

Rnd 7: Needle 1: k7 (9, 11), slip marker, k1f&b, k2; needle 2: k2, k1f&b, slip marker, k7 (9, 11); needles 3 and 4: knit—38 (46, 54) sts.

Continue in this manner, increasing on needle 1 and needle 2 every third row, until 6 (7, 8) increases have been completed and there are 14 (16, 18) thumb sts between markers—44 (54, 64) sts.

Complete mitten as for Right Mitten.

Finishing

Weave in ends.

Block mittens, if desired, according to yarn manufacturer's instructions.

Recommended Colors for Other Houses

Slytherin: Cascade *220 Superwash* #801 Army Green (color A) and #816 Gray (color B)

Ravenclaw: Cascade *220 Superwash* #813 Blue Velvet (color A) and #828 Bronze or #816 Gray (color B)

Hufflepuff: Cascade *220 Superwash* #815 Black (color A) and #820 Lemon (color B)

Materials

- Knit Picks *Essential* (75% superwash wool; 25% nylon, 231 yd. [211 m] per 50 g skein), #23698 Burgundy (color A) and Dale *Baby Ull* (100% merino wool; 180 yd. [164 m] per 50 g skein), #2317 Canary (color B):

  Wide Stripes version: 1 (1, 1, 2) skeins color A and 1 (1, 2, 2) skeins color B

  Narrow Stripes version: 1 (2, 2, 2) skeins color A and 1 skein color B

- Or similar yarn that knits to specified gauge: fingering-weight wool or wool/nylon blend:

  Wide Stripes version: About 105 (148, 204, 265) yd. [58.5 (135, 186.5, 242) m] of color A and 75 (116, 164, 221) yd. [96 (106, 150, 202) m] of color B

  Narrow Stripes version: About 156 (235, 315, 400) yd. [142.5 (215, 288, 366) m] of color A and 25 (40, 50, 65) yd. [23 (36.5, 46, 59.5) m] of color B

- US 1 [2.25 mm] double-pointed needles, set of 5
- Tapestry needle

Gauge

32 sts and 40 rnds = 4" [10 cm] in St st using size 1 [2.25 mm] needles

HOUSE SOCKS

Designer – Alison Hansel ☾
Pattern Rating – Ordinary Wizarding Level

Knitting socks is just like magic: Follow the spells, and suddenly things that didn't seem possible, like a heel, appear! This would be a great project for a new sock knitter. These cozy, top-down socks have a basic heel flap design, but because the heel is worked in a solid color, your house stripes continue neatly, uninterrupted down the entire sock. And they're knit in an economical superwash sock yarn that comes in almost every house color, so these are a bargain to make for the smallest to the biggest Harry Potter fans in your life.

Instructions

With color A, CO 48 (56, 64, 72) sts, distribute stitches so that there are 12 (14, 16, 18) sts on each of four dpns, and join in a circle, being careful not to twist sts.

Cuff

Work 1" [2.5 cm] in twisted single rib, as described in the stitch guide.

Leg

Work the leg as follows for your stripe pattern (see page 84).

Wide Stripes Pattern Only

Switch to St st and work 10 rnds in color B. Work 1 (2, 2, 3) repeats of Wide Stripes sequence described in the stripe pattern (or number of repeats required to reach desired length to heel), then work 5 rnds of color A, ending leg stripe sequence halfway through color A stripe.

Narrow Stripes Pattern Only

Switch to St st and work 2 rnds in color A, then work 2 rnds color B, 3 rnds color A, and 2 rnds color B. Work 1 (2, 2, 3) repeats of the Narrow Stripes sequence described in the stripe pattern (or number of repeats required to reach desired length to heel), then work 8 rnds of color A, ending stripe sequence halfway through large color A stripe.

Heel Flap

Sl 24 (28, 32, 36) sts from next two needles onto one needle for the heel flap. Place the rem 24 (28, 32, 36) sts (which are the instep sts) on holders or leave them on their needles.

Continuing with color A, work back and forth on the 24 (28, 32, 36) heel flap sts as follows:

Row 1 (RS): Sl 1 pwise, *k1, sl 1 kwise; rep from * to last st, k1, turn.

Row 2 (WS): Sl 1 pwise, purl to end, turn.

Rep rows 1 and 2 until heel flap measures 1¼ (1¾, 2, 2½)" [3 (4.5, 5, 6.5) cm] in length, ending with a RS row completed.

Turn Heel

Row 1 (WS): P14 (16, 18, 20), p2tog, p1. Turn, leaving rem sts on needle.

Row 2 (RS): Sl 1 pwise, k5, k2tog, k1. Turn.

Row 3: Sl 1 pwise, p6, p2tog, p1. Turn.

Row 4: Sl 1 pwise, k7, k2tog, k1. Turn.

Row 5: Sl 1 pwise, p8, p2tog, p1. Turn.

Continue in this manner—slipping the first stitch pwise, working across to 1 st before the gap, working the 2 sts on each side of the gap together to close the gap, then working 1 more st and turning the

Finished Size

S (M, L, XL)

Leg circumference: 6 (7, 8, 9)" [15 (18, 20.5, 23) cm]

Foot length: 5 (7¼, 9¼, 11)" [12.5 (18.5, 23.5, 28) cm]

Leg length (from cuff to bottom of heel flap): 5¾ (8¼, 8½, 11)" [14.5 (21, 21.5, 28) cm] for Wide Stripes version and 6¼ (9, 9¼, 12)" [16 (23, 23.5, 30.5) cm] for Narrow Stripes version

Note: Leg lengths vary slightly between the Wide Stripes and Narrow Stripes versions in order to accommodate the stripe patterns. You can easily adjust them up or down by knitting fewer or more stripe repeats.

Samples shown: Wide Stripes, size M, and Narrow Stripes, size L

Stitch Guide for This Project

Twisted Single (1x1) Rib Worked in Rounds

Rnd 1: *K1tbl, p1; rep from * to end of rnd.

Rep rnd 1.

Stockinette Stitch (St st) Worked in Rounds

Knit all sts.

Stripe Patterns

Wide Stripes

*Work 10 rnds color A, 10 rnds color B; rep from * for rest of sock.

Note: Carry yarn not in use upward at beg of each rnd for leg and foot. Cut color B yarn when working heel section and rejoin when color B stripes begin after heel.

Narrow Stripes

Work setup rnds as indicated in instructions, then *work 16 rnds color A, 2 rnds color B, 3 rnds color A, 2 rnds color B; rep from * for rest of sock.

Note: Carry color A yarn upward at beg of rnd when working color B stripe sections, but cut color B yarn when working each set 16 rnds of color A and when working the heel.

work—until all 24 (28, 32, 36) sts have been worked and 14 (16, 18, 20) heel sts rem.

Note: The last two rows for all sizes end with k2tog or p2tog, as the final sts are incorporated into the heel triangle.

Gusset

Begin working in the round again. Pick up 12 (14, 16, 18) sts along nearest side of heel flap (needle 1), k24 (28, 32, 36) instep sts (needles 2 and 3), and pick up 12 (14, 16, 18) sts along second side of heel flap (needle 4). K7 (8, 9, 10) sts (half of the heel sts) onto needle 4 just used and pm in the last st to denote end of rnd. Slip the other 7 (8, 9, 10) heel sts onto needle 1. You should now have 19 (22, 25, 28) sts on each of needles 1 and 4 and 12 (14, 16, 18) instep sts on each of needles 2 and 3—62 (72, 82, 92) sts total. Continue following chosen stripe pattern.

Note: The rnd just worked counts as your 6th rnd of color A for the Wide Stripes sequence or 9th rnd of color A for Narrow Stripes.

Gusset Decreases

Rnd 1 (dec rnd): Needle 1: knit to last 3 sts, k2tog, k1; needles 2 and 3: knit across all instep sts; needle 4: k1, ssk, knit to end of rnd—60 (70, 80, 90) sts.

Rnd 2: Knit.

Maintaining stripe patt, rep rnds 1 and 2 until 12 (14, 16, 18) sts rem on needles 1 and 4—48 (56, 64, 72) sts.

Foot

Continue in St st, without decreasing, until foot measures about 1¼ (1¾, 2¼, 2¾)" [3 (4.5, 5.5, 7) cm] shorter than desired length.

Note: The final Narrow Stripes repeat may not be complete for all sizes. The toe of the Narrow Stripes sock is worked in color A only. For Wide Stripes pattern, continue following stripe sequence as given.

Toe Decreases

Rnd 1 (dec rnd): Needle 1: knit to last 3 sts, k2tog, k1; needle 2: k1, ssk, knit to end; needle 3: knit to last 3 sts, k2tog, k1; needle 4: k1, ssk, knit to end of rnd—44 (52, 60, 68) sts.

Rnd 2: Knit.

Rep rnds 1 and 2 until 7 sts rem on each needle—28 sts. Then rep rnd 1 only until 4 sts rem on each needle—16 sts.

After completing the last rnd, remove marker, k4 sts from needle 1 onto needle 4, and slip 4 sts from needle 3 onto needle 2. At this point, there are 8 sts on needle 4 and 8 sts on needle 2.

Finishing

Cut yarn, leaving an 8" [20.5 cm] tail, and thread through tapestry needle. With the 16 sts divided on two parallel needles, use Kitchener stitch (see page 161) to graft toe sts together. Weave in ends.

Block, if desired, according to yarn manufacturer's instructions.

Make second sock the same.

Recommended Colors for Other Houses

Slytherin: Knit Picks *Essential* #23700 Pine (color A) and #23696 Ash (color B)

Ravenclaw: Knit Picks *Essential* #23694 Navy (color A) and #23696 Ash (color B)

Hufflepuff: Knit Picks *Essential* #23701 Black (color A) and Dale *Baby Ull* #2317 Canary (color B)

Materials

- Jaeger *Matchmaker Merino DK* (100% wool; 131 yd. [120 m] per 50 g ball), #639 Granite (color A), 5 (6, 7, 10, 11, 12, 15, 17) balls, and #876 Clarice (color C), 1 ball; and Jaeger *Matchmaker Merino 4-ply* (100% wool; 200 yd. [183 m] per 50 g ball), #765 Gold (color B), 1 ball

Note: The 4-ply yarn used here for color B is a finer weight than the DK yarn used, so you need to use this yarn doubled to match the gauge of the other yarn.

- Or similar yarn that knits to specified gauge: DK-weight wool or wool-blend yarn, about 580 (700, 834, 1,276, 1,433, 1,588, 1,980, 2,159) yd. [530 (640, 762, 1,167, 1,310, 1,452, 1,810, 1,974) m] of color A, 27 (28, 30, 34, 38, 41, 45, 49) yd. [24 (26, 28, 31, 35, 37, 41, 45) m] of color B, and 14 (15, 16, 17, 19, 21, 23, 25) yd. [13 (14, 14.6, 15.5, 17, 19, 21, 23) m] of color C
- US 3 [3.25 mm] needles
- US 3 [3.25 mm] 16" [40 cm] circular needle
- US 6 [4 mm] needles
- Stitch markers
- Tapestry needle

HOUSE SWEATER

Designer – Amber Daniels-Cook ☾
Pattern Rating – Ordinary Wizarding Level

A traditional v-neck school jumper with house color detailing, just like in the movies! This sweater is perfect for sending your little (or big) wizards off to school. The yarn is a classic machine-washable wool, and the flexible sizing of this sweater means everyone can have one—as long as Mrs. Weasley shares her knitting spells with you, of course!

Back

With color A and smaller needles, CO 69 (73, 79, 93, 103, 113, 123, 133) sts. Work in single rib, as described in the stitch guide, until rib measures 2" [5 cm] or desired length from CO edge, ending with a WS row completed.

Next row (RS): Knit, increasing 9 (9, 9, 11, 13, 13, 15, 15) sts, spaced evenly across row—78 (82, 88, 104, 116, 126, 138, 148) sts.

Next row (WS): Switching to larger needles, purl.

Continuing in St st, work house stripes over the next 6 rows, changing colors as described in the stripe pattern (see page 87). Cut colors B and C, leaving 8" [20.5 cm] tails.

Continuing with color A only, work even in St st until piece measures 9 (10½, 12, 14½, 15, 15½, 16½, 17)" [23 (26.5, 30.5, 37, 38, 39, 42, 43) cm] or desired length from CO edge, ending with a WS row completed.

Begin Armhole Shaping

BO 5 (6, 6, 8, 9, 10, 9, 10) sts beg next 2 rows—68 (70, 76, 88, 98, 106, 120, 128) sts.

Work decreases 1 st in from side edges, as follows:

Row 1 (dec row): K1, k2tog, knit to last 3 sts, ssk, k1.
Row 2: Purl.

Rep these 2 rows 4 (4, 5, 6, 7, 8, 8, 9) times more—58 (60, 64, 74, 82, 88, 102, 108) sts.

Work even in St st until back measures 14½ (16½, 18½, 23, 24, 25, 27½, 28½)" [37 (42, 47, 58.5, 61, 63.5, 70, 72.5) cm] or desired length from CO edge, ending with a WS row completed.

Shoulder Shaping

BO 5 (5, 5, 7, 8, 8, 9, 10) sts beg next 2 rows—48 (50, 54, 60, 66, 72, 84, 88) sts.

BO 5 (4, 5, 6, 7, 8, 9, 10) sts beg next 2 rows—38 (42, 44, 48, 52, 56, 66, 68) sts.

BO 4 (4, 5, 6, 7, 7, 9, 9) sts beg next 2 rows—30 (34, 34, 36, 38, 42, 48, 50) sts.

BO rem 30 (34, 34, 36, 38, 42, 48, 50) back neck sts.

Front

Work same as back to beg of armhole shaping.

Armhole and Neck Shaping

Counting from the right edge of the RS, place a marker on the needle after st 39 (41, 44, 52, 58, 63, 69, 74). This is the center of the row, and you should have the same number of sts on each side of the marker.

Work first 6 rows of armhole shaping same as for back—32 (33, 36, 42, 47, 51, 58, 62) sts each side of marker. Continue armhole shaping and *at the same time,* divide for neck opening as follows:

Finished Size

To fit chest: 25 (27, 28, 34, 38, 42, 46, 50)" [63.5 (68.5, 71, 86.5, 96.5, 106.5, 117, 127) cm]

Finished chest circumference: 28 (30, 32, 38, 42, 46, 50, 54)" [71 (76, 81.5, 96.5, 106.5, 117, 127, 137) cm]

Length: 15¼ (17¼, 19¼, 23¾, 24¾, 25¾, 28¼, 29¼)" [38.5 (44, 49, 60.5, 63, 65.5, 72, 74.5) cm]

Sample shown: Finished chest circumference 38" [96.5 cm]

Gauge

22 sts and 30 rows = 4" [10 cm] in St st using size 6 [4 mm] needles

Stitch Guide for This Project

Single Rib (1x1 Rib) Worked in Rows over an Odd Number of Sts

Row 1 (RS): *K1, p1; rep from * to last st, k1.

Row 2 (WS): *P1, k1; rep from * to last st, p1.

Rep rows 1 and 2.

Stockinette Stitch (St st) Worked in Rows

Row 1 (RS): Knit.

Row 2 (WS): Purl.

Rep rows 1 and 2.

Stripe Pattern

2 rows color B, 2 rows color C, 2 rows color B

Note: The yarns not in use can be cut or stranded over the rows of other colors. Be careful not to strand them so tightly that they distort the knitted fabric.

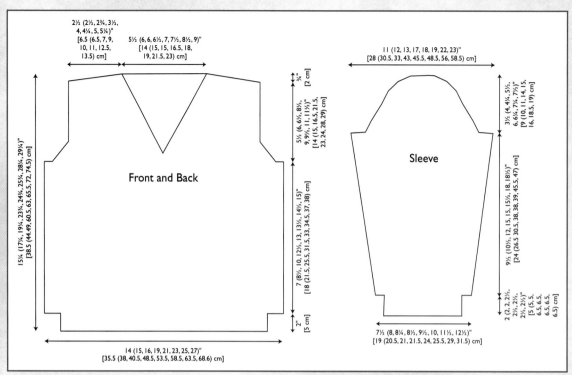

2½ (2½, 2¾, 3½, 4, 4¼, 5, 5¼)"
[6.5 (6.5, 7, 9, 10, 11, 12.5, 13.5) cm]

5½ (6, 6, 6½, 7, 7½, 8½, 9)"
[14 (15, 15, 16.5, 18, 19, 21.5, 23) cm]

11 (12, 13, 17, 18, 19, 22, 23)"
[28 (30.5, 33, 43, 45.5, 48.5, 56, 58.5) cm]

¾"
[2 cm]

5½ (6, 6½, 8½, 9, 9½, 11, 11½)"
[14 (15, 16.5, 21.5, 23, 24, 28, 29) cm]

3½ (4, 4¼, 5½, 6, 6¾, 7¼, 7½)"
[9 (10, 11, 14, 15, 16, 18.5, 19) cm]

Sleeve

Front and Back

15¼ (17¼, 19¼, 23¾, 24¾, 25¾, 28¾, 29¼)"
[38.5 (44, 49, 60.5, 63, 65.5, 72, 74.5) cm]

9½ (10½, 12, 15, 15½, 15½, 18, 18½)"
[24 (26.5, 30.5, 38, 39, 45.5, 47) cm]

7 (8½, 10, 12½, 13, 13½, 14½, 15)"
[18 (21.5, 25.5, 31.5, 33, 34.5, 37, 38) cm]

2"
[5 cm]

2 (2, 2, 2½, 2½, 2½, 2½, 2½)"
[5 (5, 5, 6.5, 6.5, 6.5, 6.5) cm]

14 (15, 16, 19, 21, 23, 25, 27)"
[35.5 (38, 40.5, 48.5, 53.5, 58.5, 63.5, 68.6) cm]

7½ (8, 8¼, 8½, 9½, 10, 11½, 12½)"
[19 (20.5, 21, 21.5, 24, 25.5, 29, 31.5) cm]

Row 7 (RS): K1, k2tog, knit to center marker, drop yarn, slip marker, attach another ball of yarn and work to last 3 sts, ssk, k1—31 (32, 35, 41, 46, 50, 57, 61) sts each side of marker.

Continue working the neck shaping according to the following directions for your size.

Note: Both sides of the front neck are worked at the same time, each with a separate ball of yarn.

Two Smallest Sizes Only

Row 8 (WS): Purl to 3 sts before center marker at neck opening, ssp, p1, drop yarn, slip marker, pick up yarn for other side of neck, p1, p2tog, purl to end—30 (31) sts each side of marker.

Row 9 (RS): K1, k2tog, knit to 3 sts before center marker at neck opening, k2tog, k1; at other neck edge k1, ssk, knit to last 3 sts, ssk, k1—28 (29) sts each side of marker.

Rows 10 and 11: Rep rows 8 and 9—25 (26) sts each side of marker.

With armhole shaping completed, continue neck shaping as follows:

Row 12 (WS): Rep row 8—24 (25) sts.

Row 13 (RS): Knit to 3 sts before neck opening, k2tog, k1; at other neck edge k1, ssk, knit to end—23 (24) sts each side of marker.

Rows 14–17: Rep rows 12 and 13 two times more—19 (20) sts each side of marker.

Row 18 (WS): Purl across both sides of neck.

Row 19 (RS): Rep row 13—18 (19) sts each side of marker.

Row 20: Rep row 18.

Rep rows 19 and 20 another 4 (6) times—14 (13) sts rem each side.

Work even in St st until front measures same as back to beg of shoulder shaping, ending with a WS row completed—14 (13) sts each side.

Six Largest Sizes

Row 8 (WS): Purl to center marker, drop yarn, slip marker, pick up yarn for other side of neck, purl to end.

Row 9 (RS): K1, k2tog, knit to 3 sts before center marker at neck opening, k2tog, k1; at other neck edge k1, ssk, knit to last 3 sts, ssk, k1— – (–, 33, 39, 44, 48, 55, 59) sts each side of marker.

Rep rows 8 and 9 another – (–, 2, 3, 4, 5, 5, 6) times— – (–, 29, 33, 36, 38, 45, 47) sts each side of marker.

With armhole shaping completed, continue neck shaping as follows:

Next row (WS): Rep row 8.

Next row (RS): Knit to 3 sts before neck opening, k2tog, k1; at other neck edge k1, ssk, knit to end— – – (–, 28, 32, 35, 37, 44, 46) sts each side of marker.

Rep last 2 rows – (–, 12, 6, 4, 6, 7, 5) times more— – – (–, 16, 26, 31, 31, 37, 41) sts each side of marker.

Next 3 rows: Beg with WS row, work even in St st on both sides of marker.

Next row (RS): Knit to 3 sts before neck opening, k2tog, k1; at other neck edge k1, ssk, knit to end— – (–, 15, 25, 30, 30, 36, 40) sts each side of marker.

Rep last 4 rows – (–, 0, 6, 8, 7, 9, 11) times more— – (–, 15, 19, 22, 23, 27, 29) sts each side of marker.

Work even in St st until front measures same as back to beg of shoulder shaping, ending with a WS row completed—14 (13, 15, 19, 22, 23, 27, 29) sts each side.

Shoulder Shaping

Row 1 (RS): BO 5 (5, 5, 7, 8, 8, 9, 10) sts at shoulder edge, knit across both sides of neck—9 (8, 10, 12, 14, 15, 18, 19) sts rem on shoulder with BO.

Row 2 (WS): BO 5 (5, 5, 7, 8, 8, 9, 10) sts at each shoulder edge, purl across both sides of neck—9 (8, 10, 12, 14, 15, 18, 19) sts rem on each shoulder.

Rows 3 and 4: BO 5 (4, 5, 6, 7, 8, 9, 10) sts beg at shoulder edge, then work in patt to end—4 (4, 5, 6, 7, 7, 9, 9) sts rem each shoulder.

Rows 5 and 6: BO rem sts beg at shoulder edge.

Cut both yarns, leaving 8" [20.5 cm] tails.

Sleeves

With color A and smaller needles, CO 37 (39, 41, 43, 47, 49, 57, 63) sts.

Work same as body rib for 2 (2, 2, 2½, 2½, 2½, 2½, 2½)" [5 (5, 5, 6.5, 6.5, 6.5, 6.5, 6.5) cm].

Row 1 (RS): Knit, increasing 5 (5, 5, 5, 5, 7, 7, 7) sts spaced evenly across row—42 (44, 46, 48, 52, 56, 64, 70) sts.

Row 2: (WS): Changing to larger needles, purl.

Note: When instructed to work RS increases, work them as follows: K1, m1, knit to last st, m1, k1.

Continuing in St st, work the stripes over the next 6 rows, changing colors as described in the stripe pattern. Cut colors B and C, leaving 8" [20.5 cm] tails. Continue in color A only.

At the same time, inc 1 st each side every 6 (6, 6, 4, 4, 4, 4, 4) rows 4 (8, 11,17, 20, 18, 23, 18) times—50 (60, 68, 82, 92, 92, 110, 106) sts.

Inc 1 st each side every 8 (8, 8, 6, 6, 6, 6, 6) rows 5 (3, 2, 6, 4, 6, 6, 10) times—60 (66, 72, 94, 100, 104, 122, 126) sts.

Work even until sleeve measures 11½ (12½, 14, 17½, 17½, 18, 20½, 21)" [29 (31.5, 35.5, 44.5, 44.5, 45.5, 52, 53.5) cm] or desired length from CO edge, ending with a WS row completed.

Cap Shaping

BO 5 (6, 6, 8, 9, 10, 9, 10) sts beg next 2 rows—50 (54, 60, 78, 82, 84, 104, 106) sts.

Next row (dec row—RS): K1, k2tog, knit to last 3 sts, ssk, k1—48 (52, 58, 76, 80, 82, 102, 104) sts.

Next row (WS): Purl.

Rep last 2 rows 4 (4, 5, 6, 7, 8, 8, 9) times more—40 (44, 48, 64, 66, 66, 86, 86) sts.

Note: Continue to work RS dec rows as before and work WS dec rows as follows: P1, ssp, purl to last 3 sts, p2tog, p1.

Dec 1 st each side every row 10 (11, 11, 14, 12, 10, 16, 13) times—20 (22, 26, 36, 42, 46, 54, 60) sts.

Dec 1 st each side every 2nd row 0 (1, 1, 4, 5, 6, 7, 9) times—20 (20, 24, 28, 32, 34, 40, 42) sts.

BO 2 (2, 3, 3, 4, 4, 5, 5) sts beg next 4 rows—12 (12, 12, 16, 16, 18, 20, 22) sts.

BO rem 12 (12, 12, 16, 16, 18, 20, 22) sts.

Make second sleeve the same.

Neckband

Backstitch (see page 159) or graft (see page 160) front to back at each shoulder. With RS facing, join color A and use circ needle to pick up 30 (34, 34, 36, 38, 42, 48, 50) sts from back neck, pick up 26 (29, 32, 43, 47, 49, 56, 61) sts along left neck edge, pm, m1 (this will be the center st), pm, pick up 26 (29, 32, 43, 47, 49, 56, 61) sts along right neck edge, and pm to denote the end of the rnd—83 (93, 99, 123, 133, 141, 161, 173) sts.

Rnd 1: Work in single rib to within 2 sts of first center marker, ssk, slip marker, k1, slip marker, k2tog, work in single rib to end of rnd.

Rnd 2: Work in established rib patt to within 2 sts of first center marker, ssk, slip marker, k1, slip marker, k2tog, work in established rib patt to end of rnd.

Rep rnd 2 until band measures 1 (1, 1, 1¼, 1¼, 1¼, 1½, 1½)" [2.5 (2.5, 2.5, 3, 3, 3, 4, 4) cm] from pick-up rnd. At this point, either remove markers, BO in rib patt, and cut yarn, leaving an 8" [20.5 cm] tail for a single-layer neckband or continue as follows to create a facing.

Facing (Optional)

Next rnd (RS): Purl next rnd (to create a turning ridge).

Next rnd: Work in established rib (following same rib patt as in rnd before turning ridge) to first center marker, m1, slip marker, k1 (center st), slip marker, m1, work in established rib to end of rnd.

Rep last rnd, working the newly made sts into the established rib patt until facing measures same as neckband and st count is the same as beg of neckband. BO all sts in rib patt. Cut yarn, leaving a 20" [51 cm] tail.

Fold facing to WS at turning ridge and pin in place.

Thread tail into a tapestry needle and whipstitch (see page 160) facing to WS along the pick-up rnd, taking care not to pull too tight. Remove pins.

Finishing

Weave in all loose ends. Block all pieces to size, according to yarn manufacturer's instructions.

When dry, sew sleeve caps into armholes, easing to fit. Use mattress stitch (see page 160) to close sleeve and side seams.

Lightly steam seams to smooth out any puckers, if necessary.

Recommended Contrast Colors for Other Houses

Slytherin: Jaeger *Matchmaker* DK #892 Putty (color B) and #730 Loden (color C)
Ravenclaw: Jaeger *Matchmaker* DK #789 Syrup (color B) and #2346 Mid Navy (color C)
Hufflepuff: Jaeger *Matchmaker* DK #681 Black (color B) and #727 Onion (color C)

Materials

- ☾ Cascade *220 Superwash* (100% superwash wool; 220 yd. [201 m] per 100 g ball), #855 Maroon (color A), 1 skein, and #821 Marigold (color B), 1 skein

- ☾ Or similar yarn that knits to specified gauge: worsted-weight wool or wool-blend yarn:

  Wide Stripes version: About 90 yd. [82 m] each of color A and color B

  Narrow Stripes version: About 120 yd. [110 m] of color A and 40 yd. [36.5 m] of color B

- ☾ US 6 [4 mm] needles
- ☾ Tapestry needle

Gauge

20 sts and 36 rows = 4" [10 cm] in garter st, using size 6 [4 mm] needles

Note: Gauge isn't terribly important in this simple scarf. You can easily adjust the number of stitches for a different gauge yarn: Cast on more stitches to use a finer yarn or fewer stitches to use a heavier yarn.

Finished Size

Width: 2" [5 cm]

Length: About 60" [152.5 cm] or desired length

HIP HOUSE SCARF

Designer – Alison Hansel ☾ *Pattern Rating – First Year*

For the hip Harry Potter fan: It's a skinny scarf, it's a tie, it's a belt, you could even wear it as a headband. Perfect for the beginning knitter, you can knit this super-simple garter stitch scarf as your very first knitting project. Or if you're an intermediate knitter, you can charm one up lickety-split before the next movie premiere. It's what all the cool Hogwarts students are wearing!

Instructions

With color A, CO 20 sts. Continuing with color A, beg following desired stripe pattern (see page 95) and work rows as follows:

Row 1 (WS): Knit.

Row 2 (RS): K2tog, knit to last st, k1f&b.

Rep rows 1 and 2, switching to color B and back to color A as described in the stripe pattern (see page 95), until scarf is approximately 60" [152.5 cm] long or desired length, ending with 10 rows of color A for Wide Stripes pattern or 14 rows of color A for Narrow Stripes pattern.

With color A, BO all stitches. Cut yarn, leaving an 8" [20.5 cm] tail.

Finishing

Weave in ends.

Block according to yarn manufacturer's instructions to prevent the scarf from curling.

Note: Although a garter stitch scarf would normally not curl, the bias shape of this scarf tends to create a slight spiral curl.

Stitch Guide for This Project

Garter Stitch Worked in Rows

Knit all sts.

Stripe Patterns

Wide Stripes

*Work 10 rows in color A, 10 rows in color B; rep from * for entire scarf, ending scarf with 10 rows of color A.

Narrow Stripes

*Work 14 rows in color A, 2 rows in color B, 2 rows in color A, 2 rows in color B; rep from * for entire scarf, ending scarf with 14 rows color A.

Note: Cut the yarn at each color change for both stripe sequences as both sides of the scarf will be visible. This makes for more ends to weave in but a much neater-looking scarf.

Recommended Colors for Other Houses

Slytherin: Cascade *220 Superwash* #801 Army Green (color A) and #816 Gray (color B)

Ravenclaw: Cascade *220 Superwash* #813 Blue Velvet (color A) and #828 Bronze or #816 Gray (color B)

Hufflepuff: Cascade *220 Superwash* #815 Black (color A) and #820 Lemon (color B)

Materials

Worsted-Weight Version

- ☾ Brown Sheep *Nature Spun Worsted* (100% wool, 245 yd. [224 m] per 100 g ball), #200 Bordeaux (color A), 1 ball, and #308 Sunburst Gold (color B), 1 ball
- ☾ Or yarn that knits to specified gauge: worsted-weight wool or wool-blend yarn:

  Wide Stripes version: About 16 yd. [14.5 m] each of color A and color B

  Narrow Stripes version: About 22 yd. [20 m] of color A and 7½ yd. [7 m] of color B

- ☾ US 7 [4.5 mm] double-pointed needles

DK-Weight Version

- ☾ Jamieson's *Double Knitting* (100% wool, 82 yd. [75 m] per 25 g ball), #168 Clyde Blue (color A), 1 ball, and #1190 Burnt Umber (color B), 1 ball
- ☾ Or yarn that knits to specified gauge: DK-weight wool or wool-blend yarn:

  Wide Stripes version: About 17¾ yd. [16 m] each of color A and color B

  Narrow Stripes version: About 25 yd. [23 m] of color A and 6 yd. [5.5 m] of color B

- ☾ US 5 [3.75 mm] double-pointed needles

HOUSE BOOKSCARVES

Designer – Laura Miller ☾ *Pattern Rating – First Year*

A large, woolly scarf isn't always practical for every climate or every season. You can make this mini version to mark your place as you reread Harry's adventures any time of the year. The Laceweight version is the perfect weight for a bookmark, but instructions are provided for two other gauges, so you can use leftovers from another House Colors project to make your bookscarf. They also make quick and simple gifts for all the Harry Potter fans in your life!

Instructions

Note: These instructions are written for the Worsted-Weight version, with changes for the DK-Weight and Laceweight versions given in parentheses. When only one number is given, it applies to all versions.

CO 16 (18, 32) sts in color A onto dpns. Divide sts as evenly as possible among needles, pm to note beg rnd, and join in a circle, being careful not to twist sts.

Work desired stripe pattern (as directed on page 98) in St st.

Note: Following the scarves in the movies, the newer, Narrow Stripes Hufflepuff scarves begin and end with yellow, so colors A and B are switched in the Narrow Stripes version for that house only. Thus, color A is yellow, and color B is black. Other house colors remain the same for both versions.

All Versions

When stripe pattern is complete, BO all sts. Cut yarn, leaving an 8" [20.5 cm] tail.

Trim tails from color changes to 1½" [4 cm] long; they can be left loose on the inside of the scarf, as they won't be seen. Leave tails from CO and BO to be incorporated into fringe.

Finishing

Flatten tube, aligning beg of rnd (where jog from color change occurs) carefully along one side edge.

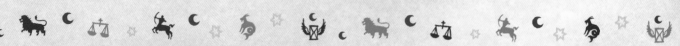

Block, if desired, according to yarn manufacturer's instructions.

Add Fringe

The Wide Stripes version and Narrow Stripes version use different fringe patterns, so follow the instructions for the appropriate version.

Wide Stripes Version

Cut 20 (20, 30) strands of color A and 16 (16, 24) strands of color B into 3" [7.5 cm] lengths.

Starting with color A, hold 2 (2, 3) strands together and fold them in half to form a loop. At one corner of either open end, use crochet hook to draw loop about halfway through both layers of bookscarf. Draw the loose ends up through loop and pull down firmly to form fringe. Space a total of 9 fringe groups across end, alternating color A and color B, as in photo.

Rep for other end.

Trim fringe to an even length.

Narrow Stripes Version

Cut 36 (36, 54) strands of color A into 1½" [4 cm] lengths.

Hold 2 (2, 3) strands together and fold them in half to form a loop. At one corner of either open end, use crochet hook to draw loop

Laceweight Version

- *Wide Stripes version:* DMC *Pearl Cotton* Size 5 (100% cotton, 27 yd. [25 m] per 5 g skein): #890 Dark Green (color A), 1 skein, and #415 Pearl Gray (color B), 1 skein

- *Narrow Stripes version:* DMC *Pearl Cotton* Size 5: #725 Topaz (color A), 2 skeins, and #310 Black (color B), 1 skein

- Or yarn that knits to specified gauge: embroidery thread or laceweight cotton or wool:

  Wide Stripes version: About 25 yd. [23 m] of color A and 12 yd. [11 m] of color B

  Narrow Stripes version: About 40 yd. [36.5 m] of color A and 15 yd. [14 m] of color B

- US 0 [2 mm] double-pointed needles

All Versions

- Stitch marker
- Tapestry needle
- Crochet hook

Gauge

Worsted-Weight Version

22 sts and 30 rnds = 4" [10 cm] in St st using size 7 [4.5 mm] needles

DK-Weight Version

26 sts and 36 rnds = 4" [10 cm] in St st using size 5 [3.75 mm] needles

Laceweight Version

43 sts and 60 rnds = 4" [10 cm] in St st using size 0 [2 mm] needles

Finished Size

Length (not including fringe): about 7–7½" [18–19 cm]

Width: 1½" [4 cm]

Note: Finished size will vary slightly, depending on chosen gauge and stripe pattern.

Stitch Guide for This Project

Stockinette Stitch (St st) Worked in Rounds

Knit all sts.

Stripe Patterns

Wide Stripes

Work 5 (6, 10) rnds color A, *5 (6, 10) rnds color B, 5 (6, 10) rnds color A; rep from * 4 times more, ending with color A.

Narrow Stripes

Work 8 (11, 16) rnds color A, *2 rnds color B, 3 (3, 4) rnds color A, 2 rnds color B, 8 (11, 16) rnds color A; rep from * 2 (2, 3) times more, ending with 8 (11, 16) rnds of color A.

Note: For each color change, do not cut yarn. Twist old color with new color at beg of first rnd of new color. Continue carrying yarn not in use loosely up the inside until the next color change.

about halfway through both layers of bookscarf. Draw the loose ends up through loop and pull down firmly to form fringe. Space a total of 9 fringe groups across end.

Rep for other end.

Trim fringe to an even length.

Recommended Colors for Other Houses

Worsted-Weight Version

Slytherin: Brown Sheep *Nature Spun Worsted* #24 Evergreen (color A) and #107 Silver Sage (color B)

Ravenclaw: Brown Sheep *Nature Spun Worsted* #36 China Blue (color A) and #94 Bev's Bear (color B)

Hufflepuff: Brown Sheep *Nature Spun Worsted* #601 Pepper (color A) and #305 Impasse Yellow (color B)

DK-Weight Version

Gryffindor: Jamieson's *Double Knitting* #595 Maroon (color A) and #425 Mustard (color B)

Slytherin: Jamieson's *Double Knitting* #800 Tartan (color A) and #125 Slate (color B)

Hufflepuff: Jamieson's *Double Knitting* #999 Black (color A) and #390 Daffodil (color B)

Laceweight Version

Gryffindor: DMC *Pearl Cotton* #815 Garnet (color A) and #976 Gold (color B)

Ravenclaw: DMC *Pearl Cotton* #796 Royal Blue (color A) and #3826 Golden Brown (color B)

The Magic of Giving

Knitting for others plays a very special role in the Harry Potter series. Mrs. Weasley gives Ron a maroon sweater every year, Ron gives it to Dobby, Dobby knits for Harry, and Hermione takes up knitting for all the house-elves! With these patterns, you can share with all these characters the joy of knitting for others.

Take a peek into Dobby's sock drawer (just don't expect to find any matching socks!), charm up a tiny elf hat, or discover the magic of felting by making Hermione's Magic Knitting Bag. You can play Mrs. Weasley and make mini-Weasley sweater ornaments for everyone at Christmas. And, in case you get into trouble, you can even knit yourself a scarf full of healing Phoenix tears.

Materials for Harry's Sock

- Knit Picks *Essential* (75% super-wash wool, 25% nylon, 231 yd. [211 m] per 50 g skein), #23701 Black, 1 (2, 2, 2) skeins
- Or similar yarn that knits to specified gauge: sock-weight wool or wool-blend yarn, about 185 (280, 355, 445) yd. [169 (256, 388, 407) m]
- US 1 [2.25 mm] double-pointed needles, set of 5
- Stitch marker
- Tapestry needle

Gauge

34 sts and 44 rnds = 4" [10 cm] in St st using size 1 [2.25 mm] needles

Finished Size

Toddler (Child S, Child L/Women S, Women L/Men S)

Leg circumference: 4¼ (5, 5¾, 6½)" [11 (12.5, 14.5, 16.5) cm] with rib relaxed

Note: Ribbing will easily expand to fit larger actual leg circumference.

Leg length (from cuff to bottom of heel): About 5 (7, 8, 9)" [12.5 (18, 20.5, 23) cm] or desired length

Foot length: About 5 (7½, 8¾, 10)" [12.5 (19, 22, 25.5) cm] or desired length

Sample shown: Child S

DOBBY'S SOCKS

Designer – Alison Hansel ☾
Pattern Rating – Ordinary Wizarding Level

Here are four single mismatched socks for kids, inspired by our favorite sock collector. There's a boy's ribbed sock based on Dobby's very first sock from Harry, a stripy girl's sock based on the mysterious pink-and-orange sock he pairs with it, and a pair with broomsticks and Snitches, just like those he knits for Harry for Christmas. Solid-color, short-row heels give these socks a neat look and provide a crisp contrast to set off the patterning on the leg and foot. And don't worry; each pattern also includes larger sizes, in case you want to knit some for yourself, too!

Note: The number of skeins and yardage given for these socks are what you need to make a matching pair. If you want to knit a mismatched pair like Dobby, you need only half this yardage amount for each sock.

Harry's Sock

Instructions

CO 48 (56, 64, 72) sts onto four dpns, pm to note beg of rnd, and join in a circle, being careful not to twist sts.

Cuff

Work in single rib, as described in the stitch guide, for 10 rnds.

Leg

Work in 3x1 rib, as described in the stitch guide, until leg measures 3 (5, 6, 7)" [7.5 (12.5, 15, 18) cm] or desired length to heel.

Heel

You'll be working the heel over the next 25 (29, 33, 37) sts in order to center the ribbing over the instep, and using wraps, as described in *Special Techniques for This Project* (see page 102), to create the short rows.

Row 1 (RS): K24 (28, 32, 36), RS wrap next st, and turn.

Row 2 (WS): P23 (27, 31, 35), WS wrap next st, and turn.

Row 3: Knit to 1 st before first wrapped st, RS wrap next st, and turn.

Row 4: Purl to 1 st before first wrapped st, WS wrap next st, and turn.

Rep rows 3 and 4 until there are 8 (9, 10, 11) wrapped sts on each side and 9 (11, 13, 15) unwrapped sts in the center.

Widen the Heel

Widening the heel involves knitting and purling wrapped stitches as described in *Special Techniques for This Project* (see page 102).

Row 1 (RS): K9 (11, 13, 15), to the first wrapped stitch, knit wrapped st, RS wrap next st (it will now have two wraps around it) and turn.

Row 2: P10 (12, 14, 16), to the first wrapped stitch, purl wrapped st, WS wrap next stitch (it will now have two wraps around it) and turn.

Row 3: Knit to the first double-wrapped stitch, knit wrapped st, RS wrap next st, and turn.

Row 4: Purl to the first double-wrapped stitch, purl wrapped st, WS wrap next st, and turn.

Stitch Guide for Harry's Sock

Single Rib (1x1 Rib) Worked in Rounds

Rnd 1: *K1, p1; rep from * to end of rnd.

Rep rnd 1.

3x1 Rib Worked in Rounds

Rnd 1: *K3, p1; rep from * to end of rnd.

Rep rnd 1.

Stockinette Stitch (St st) Worked in Rounds

Knit all sts.

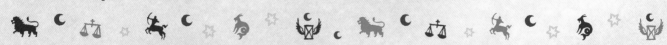

RS Wrap

Slip next st pwise, bring yarn to front between needle tips, slip st back to left needle, and bring yarn to the back between needle tips.

WS Wrap

Slip next st pwise, bring yarn to back between needle tips, slip st back to left needle, and bring yarn to the front between needle tips.

Knit Wrapped St

Insert right needle kwise into wrap(s) below st and then into the st on the needle and knit them together.

Note: When knitting a stitch together with its wrap(s), you may find it easier to pull the yarn through the st on the needle first and then, using the left needle tip, pull the wrap(s) off the right needle.

Purl Wrapped St

Insert the right needle into the wrap(s) below the st from behind (into the back of the loops) and lift the wrap(s) up onto the left needle. Purl the wrap(s) together with the next st.

Rep rows 3 and 4 until wraps have been removed from all 25 (29, 33, 37) heel sts.

Foot

K12 (14, 16, 18) and pm to mark new beg of rnd.

Begin working in the round again, working all heel/sole sts in St st and continuing ribbing as established over 23 (27, 31, 35) instep sts. Continue until foot measures about 1½ (1½, 1¾, 1¾)" [4 (4, 4.5, 4.5) cm] shorter than desired foot length.

Toe

The short-row toe is worked just as the short-row heel but over 24 (28, 32, 36) sts—the 12 (14, 16, 18) sts before the beg of the rnd and 12 (14, 16, 18) sts after the beg of the rnd.

Row 1 (RS): K11 (13, 15, 17), RS wrap next st, and turn.

Row 2 (WS): P22 (26, 30, 34), WS wrap next st, and turn.

Row 3: Knit to 1 st before first wrapped st, RS wrap next st, and turn.

Row 4: Purl to 1 st before first wrapped st, WS wrap next st, and turn.

Rep rows 3 and 4 until there are 8 (9, 10, 11) wrapped sts on each side and 8 (10, 12, 14) unwrapped sts in the center.

Widen the Toe

Row 1 (RS): K8 (10, 12, 14), to the first wrapped stitch, knit wrapped st, RS wrap next st (it will now have two wraps around it) and turn.

Row 2 (WS): P9 (11, 13, 15), to the first wrapped stitch, purl wrapped st, WS wrap next st (it will now have two wraps around it) and turn.

Row 3: Knit to first double-wrapped stitch, knit wrapped st, RS wrap next st, and turn.

Row 4: Purl to first double-wrapped stitch, purl wrapped st, WS wrap next st, and turn.

Rep rows 3 and 4 until wraps have been removed from all 24 (28, 32, 36) sts.

When toe is complete, place all 24 (28, 32, 36) toe sts on one needle. Place rem 24 (28, 32, 36) sts from instep on second needle.

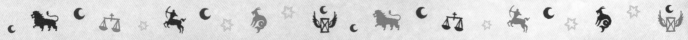

Finishing

Cut yarn, leaving a 10" [25.5 cm] tail and, using Kitchener stitch (see page 162), graft toe together.

Pull yarn to the inside of sock and weave in ends.

Block, if desired, according to yarn manufacturer's instructions.

Pink & Orange Striped Sock

Instructions

With orange, CO 48 (56, 64, 72) sts onto four dpns, pm to note beg of rnd, and join in a circle, being careful not to twist sts.

Cuff

Work in single rib, as described in the stitch guide (see page 104), for 10 rnds.

Leg

Changing to St st and beg color sequence described in the stripe pattern (see page 104), work until leg measures about 3 (5, 6, 7)" [7.5 (12.5, 15, 18) cm] from CO edge, or desired length to heel, having completed 2 rnds of pink. Cut orange yarn.

Heel

The short-row heel is worked in pink over 24 (28, 32, 36) sts—the 12 (14, 16, 18) sts before the beg of the rnd and the 12 (14, 16, 18) sts after the beg of the rnd. Work short-row heel following the instructions for the short-row *toe* for Harry's Sock, page 102.

Foot

When heel is complete, rejoin orange yarn, K12 (14, 16, 18), and pm to note new beg of rnd.

Begin working in the round again and, continuing stripe sequence, work in St st until foot measures about 1½ (1½, 1¾, 1¾)" [4 (4, 4.5,

Materials for Pink & Orange Striped Sock

- Dale *Baby Ull* (100% merino wool, 180 yd. [164 m] per 50 g skein): #2908 Orange, 1 (1, 2, 2) skeins, and #4504 Pink, 1 (1, 1, 2) skeins
- Or similar yarn that knits to specified gauge: sock-weight wool or wool-blend yarn, about 100 (147, 188, 243) yd. [91.5 (134, 172, 222) m] of orange yarn and 80 (117,168, 203) yd. [73 (107, 153.5, 185.5) m] of pink yarn
- US 1 [2.25 mm] double-pointed needles, set of 5
- Stitch marker
- Tapestry needle

Gauge

34 and 44 rnds = 4" [10 cm] in St st using size 1 [2.25] needles

Finished Size

Toddler (Child S, Child L/Women S, Women L/Men S)

Leg circumference: 5½ (6½, 7½, 8½)" [14 (16.5, 19, 21.5) cm]

Leg length (from cuff to bottom of heel): About 5 (7, 8, 9)" [12.5 (18, 20.5, 23) cm] or desired length

Foot length: About 5 (7½, 8¾, 10)" [12.5 (19, 22, 25.5) cm] or desired length

Sample shown: Child S

Stitch Guide for Pink & Orange Striped Sock

Single Rib (1x1 Rib) Worked in Rounds

Rnd 1: *K1, p1; rep from * to end of rnd.

Rep rnd 1.

Stockinette Stitch (St st) Worked in Rounds

Knit all sts.

Stripe Pattern

*2 rnds pink; 2 rnds orange; rep from * as instructed for entire leg and foot.

Note: The yarn not in use can be stranded upward up the inside of the sock at the beg of each rnd but should be cut over the heel.

Materials for Broomsticks Sock

- ☾ Dale *Baby Ull* (100% merino wool 180 yd. [164 m] per 50 g skein), #4227, Red (color A), 2 (2, 2, 3) skeins, and Knit Picks *Essential* (75% superwash wool, 25% nylon, 231 yd. [211 m] per 50 g skein), #23697 Cocoa (color B), 1 skein, and #23692 Fawn (color C), 1 skein
- ☾ Or similar yarn that knits to specified gauge: sock-weight wool or wool-blend yarn, about 190 (290, 350, 480) yd. [174 (265, 320, 439) m] of color A and 5 (10, 12, 14) yd. [4.5 (9, 11, 13) m] each of colors B and C
- ☾ US 1 [2.25 mm] double-pointed needles, set of 5
- ☾ Stitch marker
- ☾ Tapestry needle

4.5) cm] shorter than desired foot length, ending 12 (14, 16, 18) sts before end of second rnd of pink. Join orange yarn and work rem 12 (14, 16, 18) sts of rnd with orange. Cut pink yarn.

Toe

Using orange yarn, work short-row toe the same as the short-row toe for Harry's Sock, page 102.

Finishing

When toe is complete, finish sock as directed for Harry's Sock, page 103.

Broomsticks Sock

Instructions

With color A, CO 56 (64, 72, 80) sts onto four dpns, pm to note beg rnd, and join in a circle, being careful not to twist sts.

Note: To compensate for the extra thickness of the stranded colorwork, the leg of this sock has more sts than the first two socks in this pattern. The stitch count is decreased before the heel is begun.

Cuff

Work in single rib, as described in the stitch guide (see page 105), for 10 rnds.

Leg

Note: The leg length is adjusted for each size by working different numbers of repeats of the charted motif. Solid color rows are worked before and after to separate the repeats and to center the motifs on the leg.

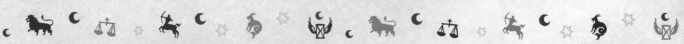

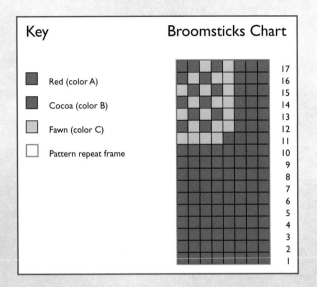

Key

■ Red (color A)

■ Cocoa (color B)

■ Fawn (color C)

□ Pattern repeat frame

Broomsticks Chart

17 16 15 14 13 12 11 10 9 8 7 6 5 4 3 2 1

You can adjust the leg length by working a different number of chart repeats or by working more/fewer solid color rows before, between, or after the motifs.

Work in St st for 4 rnds. Then, referring to chart (see page 105), continue in St st and work patt as follows:

Rnds 1–17: *Work 8 sts of chart; rep from * to end of rnd.

Toddler Size Only

For Toddler size only, after rnd 17 is completed, cut yarns B and C and go to *Decrease: For All Sizes*, page 106.

All Sizes Except Toddler

After rnd 17 is completed, continue for all sizes except Toddler as follows:

Rnds 18–20: With color A, knit.

Rnds 21–37: Work last 4 sts of chart, *work 8 sts of chart; rep from * to last 4 sts, work first 4 sts of chart.

Child S and Child L/Women S Only

For Child S and Child L/Women S sizes only, after rnd 37 is completed, cut yarns B and C and go to *Decrease: For All Sizes*, page 106.

Gauge

34 sts and 44 rnds = 4" [10 cm] in St st using size 1 [2.25 mm] needles

Note: When working the motifs on the leg, be careful not to strand yarn too tightly across the back, or your gauge will be affected, and the sock may be too tight to wear.

Finished Size

Toddler (Child S, Child L/ Women S, Women L/Men S)

Leg circumference: 6½ (7½, 8½, 9½)" [16.5 (19, 21.5, 24) cm]

Note: Because of the stranded colorwork, these socks have very little stretch.

Leg length (from cuff to bottom of heel): About 5 (7, 7, 9)" [12.5 (18, 18, 23) cm] or desired length

Foot length: About 5 (7½, 8¾,10)" [12.5 (19, 22, 25.5) cm] or desired length

Sample shown: Child S

Stitch Guide for Broomsticks Sock

Single Rib (1x1 Rib) Worked in Rounds

Rnd 1: *K1, p1; rep from * to end of rnd.

Rep rnd 1.

Stockinette Stitch (St st) Worked in Rounds

Knit all sts.

Women L/Men S Only

After rnd 37 is completed, continue for Women L/Men S as follows:

Rnds 38–40: With color A, knit.

Rnds 41–57: Rep rnds 1–17.

Cut yarns B and C and go to *Decrease: For All Sizes,* below.

Decrease: For All Sizes

Continuing with color A only, decrease sts as follows:

Rnds 1 and 3: Knit.

Rnd 2 (dec rnd): *K12 (14, 16, 18), k2tog; rep from * to end of rnd—52 (60, 68, 76) sts.

Rnd 4 (dec rnd): *K11 (13, 15, 17), k2tog; rep from * to end of rnd—48 (56, 64, 72) sts.

Heel

The short-row heel is worked in color A over 24 (28, 32, 36) sts—the 12 (14, 16, 18) sts before the beg of the rnd and the 12 (14, 16, 18) sts after the beg of the rnd. Work short-row heel following the instructions for the short-row *toe* for Harry's Sock, page 102.

Foot

When heel is complete, k12 (14, 16, 18) and pm to mark new beg of rnd.

Begin working in the round again, continuing in St st, until foot measures about 1½ (1½, 1¾, 1¾)" [4 (4, 4.5, 4.5) cm] shorter than desired foot length.

Toe

Work short-row toe the same as the short-row toe for Harry's Sock, page 102.

Finishing

When toe is complete, finish sock as directed for Harry's Sock, page 103.

Snitches Sock

Instructions

With color A, CO 56 (64, 72, 80) sts onto four dpns, pm to note beg rnd, and join in a circle, being careful not to twist sts.

Note: To compensate for the extra thickness of the stranded colorwork, the leg of this sock has more sts than the first two socks in this pattern. The stitch count is decreased before the heel is begun.

Cuff

Work in single rib, as described in the stitch guide (see page 108), for 10 rnds.

Leg

Note: The leg length is adjusted for each size by working different numbers of repeats of the charted motif. Solid color rows are worked before and after to separate the repeats and to center the motifs on the leg. You can adjust the leg length by working a different number of chart repeats or by working more/fewer solid color rows before, between, or after the motifs.

Work in St st for 4 rnds. Then, referring to the chart on page 108, continue in St st and work patt as follows:

Rnds 1–13: *Work 8 sts of chart; rep from * to end of rnd.

Toddler Size Only

For Toddler size only, after rnd 13 is completed, cut yarns B and C and go to *Decrease: For All Sizes,* page 108.

All Sizes Except Toddler

After rnd 13 is completed, continue for all sizes except Toddler as follows:

Rnds 14–20: With color A, knit.

Rnds 21–33: Work last 4 sts of chart, *work 8 sts of chart; rep from * to last 4 sts, work first 4 sts of chart.

Materials for Snitches Sock

- Knit Picks *Essential* (75% superwash wool, 25% nylon, 231 yd. [211 m] per 50 g skein), #23700 Pine (color A), 1 (1, 2, 2) skeins, and #23692 Fawn (color C), 1 skein, and Jaeger *Matchmaker Merino 4 ply* (100% merino wool, 200 yd. [183 m] per 50 g skein), #756 Gold (color B), 1 skein

- Or similar yarn that knits to specified gauge: sock-weight wool or wool-blend yarn, about 190 (290, 350, 480) yd. [173 (265, 320, 439) m] of color A, 7 (16, 18, 20) yd. [6.5 (14.5, 16.5, 18) m] of color B, and 3½ (8, 9, 10) yd. [3 (7, 8, 9) m] of color C

- US 1 [2.25 mm] double-pointed needles, set of 5

- Stitch marker

- Tapestry needle

Gauge

34 sts and 44 rnds = 4" [10 cm] in St st using size 1 [2.25 mm] needles

Note: When working the motifs on the leg, be careful not to strand yarn too tightly across the back, or your gauge will be affected, and the sock may be too tight to wear.

Finished Size

Toddler (Child S, Child L/
Women S, Women L/Men S)

Leg circumference: 6½ (7½, 8½,
9½)" [16.5 (19, 21.5, 24) cm]

Note: Because of the stranded
colorwork, these socks have very
little stretch.

Leg length (from cuff to bottom of
heel): About 5 (7, 7, 9)" [12.5 (18,
18, 23) cm] or desired length

Foot length: About 5 (7½, 8¾,10)"
[12.5 (19, 22, 25.5) cm] or desired
length

Sample shown: Child S

Stitch Guide for Snitches Sock

**Single Rib (1x1 Rib) Worked
in Rounds**

Rnd 1: *K1, p1; rep from * to end
of rnd.

Rep rnd 1.

**Stockinette Stitch (St st)
Worked in Rounds**

Knit all sts.

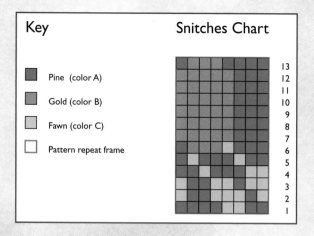

Key

Snitches Chart

- ⬛ Pine (color A)
- 🟫 Gold (color B)
- ⬜ Fawn (color C)
- ☐ Pattern repeat frame

Child S and Child L/Women S Only

For Child S and Child L/Women S sizes only, after rnd 33 is completed, cut yarns B and C and go to *Decrease: For All Sizes,* below.

Women L/Men S Only

After rnd 33 is completed, continue for Women L/Men S as follows:

Rnds 34–40: With color A, knit.

Rnds 41–53: Rep rnds 1–13.

Cut yarns B and C and go to *Decrease: For All Sizes,* below.

Decrease: For All Sizes

Continuing with color A only, decrease sts as follows:

Rnds 1–3: Knit.

Rnd 4 (dec rnd): *K12 (14, 16, 18), k2tog; rep from * to end of rnd—52 (60, 68, 76) sts.

Rnds 5–7: Rep rnds 1–3.

Rnd 8: *K11 (13, 15, 17), k2tog; rep from * to end of rnd—48 (56, 64, 72) sts.

Heel

The short-row heel is worked in color A over 24 (28, 32, 36) sts—the 12 (14, 16, 18) sts before the beg of the rnd and the 12 (14, 16, 18) sts after the beg of the rnd. Work short-row heel following the instructions for the short-row *toe* for Harry's Sock, page 102.

Foot

When heel is complete, k12 (14, 16, 18) and pm to mark new beg of rnd.

Begin working in the round again, continuing in St st, until foot measures about 1½ (1½, 1¾, 1¾)" [4 (4, 4.5, 4.5) cm] shorter than desired foot length.

Toe

Work short-row toe the same as the short-row toe for Harry's Sock, page 102.

Finishing

When toe is complete, finish sock as directed for Harry's sock, page 103.

Materials for Tea Cozy Crown

- ☾ Classic Elite *Bazic Wool* (100% superwash wool; 65 yd. [60 m] per 50 g ball), #2945 Suede (color A), 1 (2, 2) balls, and #2902 Wintergreen (color B), 1 ball

- ☾ Or similar yarn that knits to specified gauge: heavy worsted/Aran-weight wool or wool-blend yarn, about 65 (88, 115) yd. [59.5 (80.5, 105) m] of color A and 13 yd. [12 m] of color B

- ☾ US 8 [5 mm] needles

- ☾ Tapestry needle

Gauge

16 sts and 36 rows = 4" [10 cm] in garter st using size 8 [5 mm] needles

Finished Size

S (M, L)

Circumference: 16 (18, 20)" [40.5 (45.5, 51) cm]

Length: 4½ (5½, 6½)" [11.5 (14, 16.5) cm]

Sample shown: Size S

Stitch Guide for This Pattern

Garter Stitch (Garter st) Worked in Rows

Knit all sts.

ELF HATS

Designer – Alison Hansel ☾ Pattern Rating – First Year

Inspired by Hermione's extracurricular knitting endeavors, here are three unique and quirky hats for the little house-elves in your life! Perfect for the adventurous beginning knitter and little heads in need of uncommon toppers, these are knit in a large gauge and a colorful superwash yarn. One ball of the main color is just enough to make the smallest size (for babies or, when worn slightly above the ears, even toddlers)!

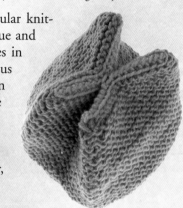

Tea Cozy Crown

Dobby would feel like a king in a tea cozy hat like this one. This easy-to-knit hat is worked flat in garter stitch. The magic is in the seaming at the top.

Instructions

With color A, CO 64 (72, 80) sts, leaving a 10" [25.5 cm] tail for seaming.

Work in garter st, as described in the stitch guide, for 17 (21, 25) rows.

Drop color A (do not cut), switch to color B, and work 6 rows in garter st.

Cut color B, leaving tail to weave in later, pick up color A again, and work 19 (23, 27) rows in garter st.

Cut color A, leaving tail to weave in later, and rejoin color B.

BO all sts with color B. Cut yarn, leaving a 24" [61 cm] tail for seaming top.

Finishing

Fold hat in half with RS facing you. (*Note:* The side that shows three color B stripes—two thin and one thick—as shown in the photos, should be on the outside.) Using color B strand still attached at end of BO row, whipstitch first and last 8 (9, 10) sts of BO edge together on the RS so that sts are visible.

Count out next 16 (18, 20) sts of BO edge along one side. Fold those sts in half and, continuing in color B, whipstitch together. Bring yarn to inside of hat and weave in underneath those sts just sewn together to bring yarn back to center opening. Rep from * to * once more, then fold last 16 (18, 20) BO sts in half and whipstitch together.

Bring yarn through center opening and weave in all ends except tail from CO. With CO tail threaded on tapestry needle, sew side seam and weave in end.

Block, if desired, according to yarn manufacturer's instructions.

Materials for Gryffindor Common Room Cap

- ☾ Classic Elite *Bazic Wool* (100% superwash wool; 65 yd. [60 m] per 50 g ball): #2958 Barn Red (color A), 1 (2, 2) balls, and #2925 Sunflower (color B), 1 ball

- ☾ Or similar yarn that knits to specified gauge: heavy worsted/Aran-weight wool or wool-blend yarn, about 65 (90, 112) yd. [59 (82, 102) m] of color A and 12 yd. [11 m] of color B

- ☾ US 8 [5 mm] 16" [40 cm] circular needle for sizes M and L

- ☾ US 8 [5 mm] double-pointed needles

Note: For size S, which is too small to work on a 16" [40 cm] circular needle, you can use either double-pointed needles or a 11½ or 12" [29 or 30.5 cm] circular needle and double-pointed needles.

- ☾ Stitch marker
- ☾ Tapestry needle
- ☾ Stitch holder or spare double-pointed or circular needle to hold triangles

Gauge

17 sts and 24 rnds = 4" [10 cm] in St st using size 8 [5 mm] needles

Gryffindor Common Room Cap

Liberating the Hogwarts house-elves, one cap at a time! Don't stay up too late at night knitting these delightful wizard-style hats for the elves in your house.

Instructions

Make Triangles

With color B, CO 1 st.

> **Row 1:** K1f&b—2 sts.
> **Row 2:** K1f&b, knit to end—3 sts.

Rep row 2 until you have 10 (12, 14) sts. Cut yarn, leaving an 8" [20.5 cm] tail to weave in later, and slip triangle onto stitch holder or spare needle.

Make two more triangles with color B. Make three triangles with color A. Do not cut yarn when finished with the last color A triangle.

Join Triangles

Place all triangles on circular needle behind the triangle already on the needle, arranging each like the beg color A triangle, with final yarn tail to the right in position to knit next row. Alternate one color A triangle, one color B triangle, and so on, ending with a color B triangle. You should have a total of 60 (72, 84) sts.

Beginning next round at right edge of last color A triangle and using color A yarn still attached, knit across all sts. When you return to the first color A triangle, pm, join in a circle, being careful not to twist sts, and purl 1 rnd.

Continuing with color A, work in St st until hat measures 2¾" [7 cm] from triangle joins (purl round).

Decrease for Top

Changing to dpns when there are too few sts to continue on circ needle, work decreases as follows:

> **Rnd 1:** *K8 (10, 12), k2tog; rep from * to end of rnd—54 (66, 78) sts.
> **Rnds 2, 3, 5, 6, 8, 9, 11, 12, 14, 15, 17, and 18:** Knit.

Rnd 4: *K7 (9, 11), k2tog; rep from * to end of rnd—48 (60, 72) sts.

Rnd 7: *K6 (8, 10), k2tog; rep from * to end of rnd—42 (54, 66) sts.

Rnd 10: *K5 (7, 9), k2tog; rep from * to end of rnd—36 (48, 60) sts.

Rnd 13: *K4 (6, 8), k2tog; rep from * to end of rnd—30 (42, 54) sts.

Rnd 16: *K3 (5, 7), k2tog; rep from * to end of rnd—24 (36, 48) sts.

Rnd 19: *K2 (4, 6), k2tog; rep from * to end of rnd—18 (30, 42) sts.

For size S, go to *Final Decreases: All Sizes,* below. For sizes M and L, continue decreasing, as follows.

Sizes M and L Only

Continue decreases for sizes M and L as follows:

Rnds 20, 21, 23, and 24: Knit.

Rnd 22: *K– (3, 5), k2tog; rep from * to end of rnd— – (24, 36) sts.

Rnd 25: *K– (2, 4), k2tog; rep from * to end of rnd— – (18, 30) sts.

For size M, go to *Final Decreases: All Sizes,* below.

Size L Only

Continue decreases for size L as follows:

Rnds 26, 27, 29, and 30: Knit.

Rnd 28: *K– (–, 3), k2tog; rep from * to end of rnd— – (–, 24) sts.

Rnd 31: *K– (–, 2), k2tog; rep from * to end of rnd— – (–, 18) sts.

Final Decreases: All Sizes

Switch to color B and work final decreases as follows:

Rnds 1, 2, 4, and 5: Knit.

Rnd 3: *K1, k2tog; rep from * to end of rnd—12 sts.

Rnd 6: *K2tog; rep from * to end of rnd—6 sts.

Finished Size

S (M, L)

Circumference: 14 (17, 19¾)" [35.5 (43, 50) cm]

Length: 9 (10, 11)" [23 (25.5, 28) cm]

Sample shown: Size S

Stitch Guide for Gryffindor Common Room Cap

Garter Stitch (Garter st) Worked in Rows

Knit all sts.

Stockinette Stitch (St st) Worked in Rounds

Knit all sts.

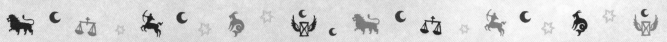

Finishing

Cut yarn, leaving an 8" [20.5 cm] tail. Thread tail through rem sts to close top of hat.

Weave in ends.

Block, if desired, according to yarn manufacturer's instructions.

Materials for Twisted Pumpkin

- ☾ Classic Elite *Bazic Wool* (100% superwash wool, 65 yd. [60 m] per 50 g ball), #2985 Marigold, 1 (2, 2) balls
- ☾ Or similar yarn that knits to specified gauge: heavy worsted/Aran-weight wool or wool-blend yarn, about 65 (85, 110) yd. [60 (78,100) m]
- ☾ US 8 [5 mm] 16" [40 cm] circular needle for sizes M and L
- ☾ US 8 [5 mm] double-pointed needles

Note: For size S, which is too small to work on a 16" [40 cm] circular needle, you can use either double-pointed needles or a 11½ or 12" [29 or 30.5 cm] circular needle and double-pointed needles.

- ☾ Stitch marker
- ☾ Tapestry needle

Gauge

17 sts and 24 rnds = 4" [10 cm] in bias rib using size 8 [5 mm] needles

Finished Size

S (M, L)
Circumference: 14 (17, 19¾)" [35.5 (43, 50) cm]
Length: 7 (8, 9)" [18 (20.5, 23) cm]

Sample shown: Size S

Twisted Pumpkin

Everyone at Hogwarts loves Halloween! Celebrate Halloween all year 'round with this twist on a popular child's hat pattern.

Instructions

With circ needle CO 60 (72, 84) sts, pm to note beg of rnd, and join in a circle, being careful not to twist sts.

Edging

Work edging in rev St st, as described in the stitch guide, for 3 rnds.

Body

Establish bias rib patt:

Setup rnd: *K5, p1; rep from * to end of rnd.

Work bias rib patt, as described in the stitch guide, until hat measures 4 (5, 6)" [10 (12.5, 15) cm], ending with a rnd 1 completed.

Decrease for Top

Changing to dpns when there are too few sts to continue on circ needle, work decreases as follows:

Rnd 1: *K2tog, k3, p1; rep from * to end of rnd—50 (60, 70) sts.

Rnd 2: *K2tog, k2, k1f&b; rep from * to end of rnd—50 (60, 70) sts.

Rnd 3: *K2tog, k2, p1; rep from * to end of rnd—40 (48, 56) sts.

Rnd 4: *K2tog, k1, k1f&b; rep from * to end of rnd—40 (48, 56) sts.

Rnd 5: *K2tog, k1, p1; rep from * to end of rnd—30 (36, 42) sts.

Rnd 6: *K2tog, k1f&b; rep from * to end of rnd—30 (36, 42) sts.

Reverse Stockinette Stitch (rev St st) Worked in Rounds
Purl all sts.

Bias Rib

Rnd 1: *K2tog, k3, k1f&b; rep from * to end of rnd.

Rnd 2: *K5, p1; rep from * to end of rnd.

Rep rows 1 and 2.

Rnd 7: *K2tog, p1; rep from * to end of rnd—20 (24, 28) sts.

Rnd 8: *K2tog, leave st on left needle, knit into back of st; rep from * to end of rnd—20 (24, 28) sts.

Rnd 9: *K2tog, k1, p1; rep from * to end of rnd—15 (18, 21) sts.

Rnd 10: *K2tog, k1f&b; rep from * to end of rnd—15 (18, 21) sts.

Rnd 11: *K2tog, p1; rep from * to end of rnd—10 (12, 14) sts.

Rnd 12: *K2tog, leave st on left needle, knit into back of st; rep from * to end of rnd—10 (12, 14) sts.

Rnd 13: *K1, p1; rep from * to end of rnd—10 (12, 14) sts.

Rep last 2 rnds 2 times more.

Finishing

Cut yarn, leaving an 8" [20.5 cm] tail. Thread tail through rem sts to close top of hat.

Weave in ends.

Block, if desired, according to yarn manufacturer's instructions.

Materials

- ☾ Cascade *220* (100% wool; 220 yd. [201 m] per 100 g skein): #8555 Black (color A), 4 skeins, and #9467 Cornflower (color B), 3 skeins
- ☾ Or similar yarn that knits to specified gauge: worsted-weight wool or other yarn that felts, about 1,540 yd. [1,410 m] total

Note: This bag is a great project to use up all your wooly leftovers from other projects. As long as the yarns you choose are either at least 60% wool (preferably 100% wool) or, in the case of novelty yarns, carried with a wool yarn, the bag will felt successfully. Keep in mind that superwash wool yarn is specially treated so that it does not felt.

- ☾ 3 yd. [2.75 m] crochet cotton or other yarn that will not felt
- ☾ US 15 [10 mm] 24–32" [60–80 cm] circular needle
- ☾ US 11 [8 mm] 24–32" [60–80 cm] circular needle
- ☾ US J [6 mm] crochet hook
- ☾ Stitch markers
- ☾ Tapestry needle
- ☾ 2 yd. [1.83 m] nylon webbing for strap (available in sewing and craft stores)
- ☾ Sewing needle
- ☾ Strong nylon (upholstery) thread

HERMIONE'S MAGIC KNITTING BAG

Designer – Shannon Okey ☾ *Pattern Rating – First Year*

This striped bag is big enough to hold your knitting projects for all your favorite house-elves, as well as your schoolbooks, lunch, magic wands . . . you name it! It's knit almost entirely in the round, which means next to no purling, and then it's felted for durability. This pattern is very flexible: You can knit it as a schoolbag in your house colors, or using leftovers from other projects, and you can adjust the size easily. Make up your own stripe pattern, and watch the felting process magically transform it!

Instructions

Note: The bag flap is knit first in rows, then stitches are cast on to form the bag body, which is knit from the top down, in rounds. Once the bag body is done, stitches are bound off on all but one edge, and the bag bottom is knit back and forth in garter st. After the bottom is sewn closed, the bag is felted in the washing machine. Straps are added after the felting.

Flap

With larger needle and color A, CO 75 sts. Beginning with a RS row, work St st in rows until piece measures 20" [51 cm]. End with a RS row completed.

Bag Body

Turn flap so that the WS is facing and pm. Using cable cast-on (see page 154), CO 35 sts, pm, CO 75 sts, pm, CO 35 sts, pm—220 sts.

Note: The last marker placed is the beginning of the round. You may want to use a different color or style of stitch marker here.

Turn work back to RS and join in a circle, being careful not to twist sts.

Work St st in rnds, following stripe pattern on page 118 or switching colors every few rows according to your own stripe plan until the bag body

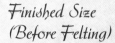

measures 20" [51 cm] from where you joined to work in the round (or twice as tall as you would like the finished bag to be).

Note: Felted items shrink more vertically than they do horizontally: Depending on your yarn and washing machine, felted items may lose from 30% to 60% of their height but shrink only about 10% to 15% widthwise. So if you'd like wider stripes or a deeper bag, knit more rounds.

Final rnd: Remove marker, k75; BO 35 sts, remove marker; BO 75 sts, remove marker; BO 35 sts, remove marker—75 sts rem.

The rem 75 sts form the bottom of the bag.

Bottom

Note: Bag bottoms tend to get dusty and dirty very easily, so use a dark color or one that will hide dirt!

With color A, switch to smaller needle and work garter st in rows until piece is long enough to fill in the bottom of the bag (approximately 40 garter ridges, but this may vary based on your gauge and yarns used). BO all sts.

Finishing

Using a crochet hook and color A, turn the bag inside out and use crochet sl st (see page 159) to join the three open sides of the bag's bottom to the upper portion of the bag, forming the sides, front, and back.

Note: Instead of using a crochet hook and sl st, you could instead seam the bag together using a tapestry needle; however, the crocheted seams are thicker and tend to create a more durable join when the bag is felted.

To give the illusion of side seams, with a crochet hook and color B, join yarn and sc (see page 158) along the flap's outer edges and down the side panels of the bag. To position this correctly, crochet into the vertical line of stitches directly below each corner where the flap meets

Finished Size (Before Felting)

Width: approx 19–20" [48–50 cm]

Height: approx 20" [46 cm]

Note: Finished size will vary based on yarn used, gauge, and amount of felting.

Sample shown: Felted size 15" [38 cm] wide and 8½" [21.5 cm] high

Gauge

Before felting: 16 sts = 4" [10 cm] in St st using size 15 [10 mm] needles

Note: Gauge is not critical to this pattern as the felting will "erase" the stitches and make a solid fabric. You simply want to make sure that you do not have any large holes anywhere in your knitted piece. If you find that you are getting fewer than 16 sts to 4" [10 cm], switch to the next smaller needle size.

Stitch Guide for This Project

Stockinette Stitch (St st) Worked in Rows

Row 1 (RS): Knit.

Row 2 (WS): Purl.

Rep rows 1 and 2.

Stockinette Stitch (St st) Worked in Rnds

Knit all sts.

Garter Stitch (Garter st) Worked in Rows

Knit all sts.

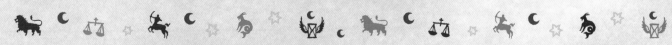

Stripe Pattern

Work 7 rnds color B, 8 rnds color A, 7 rnds color B, 8 rnds color A, 7 rnds color B, 4 rnds color A, 2 rnds color B, 4 rnds color A, 4 rnds color B, 6 rnds color A.

Note: Have fun making up your own stripe sequence. Start with a swatch to try out your own ideas. Be sure to felt your swatch to see what it will look like when the bag is finished. Use more colors, make more stripes, whatever!

the bag body. Count 35 sts across a side panel from one corner and crochet into that vertical line of stitches. Count 75 sts across the front from that vertical line and crochet down that vertical line of stitches.

To keep the bag flap from deforming during the felting process, whipstitch the front of the bag flap to the front of the bag body using crochet cotton or another yarn that will not felt and big stitches that will be easy to pick out later.

Felting

Set your washing machine to heavy-duty or similar cycle (hot wash, cold rinse), place your knitted bag in the washer inside a zippered lingerie bag or zippered pillowcase to keep lint from collecting in your washing machine, and wash with a little dish soap or laundry detergent to felt. Watch the bag during the initial agitation cycle. If you can still see individual stitches, reset the machine to go through a second agitation cycle. (Don't let the cold rinse water hit it yet!) When the bag has felted completely and you cannot see the individual stitches any longer, allow it to go through the cold rinse cycle.

Remove the whipstitching from the flap and stuff the bag with an appropriately sized cardboard box, newspaper, or plastic bags to shape it while it dries.

When the bag is dry, trim any loose yarn ends.

Adding a Strap

Cut nylon webbing to the strap length you prefer.

Center one end of strap on one side of bag and stitch it in place with strong nylon thread and a sewing needle. Bring top edges of side panel tog over strap, folding fabric from both sides of strap over the strap to cover it. (This creates a gusset.) Stitch into place. Stitch corners of bag to corners of fabric covering strap.

Repeat for the other end of the strap.

Note: Now that your fabric is felted, the stitches are no longer "live"— that is, if you cut the fabric, it won't unravel. If your flap is longer than you want it to be, you can trim it with scissors to any length you want. Fill the bag with newspaper or plastic bags before you trim so that you can accurately see how the flap will fall.

HARRY CHRISTMAS ORNAMENTS

Designer – Alison Hansel ☾ Pattern Rating – First Year

You'll have a magical Christmas tree with these two very merry (and very Harry) tree ornaments: mini-Weasley sweaters and golden Snitch balls, each with their own hangers. Making these ornaments is a great way to transfigure some leftover yarn into something special!

Mini-Weasley Sweater Ornaments

Knit in a rustic heathered wool, these mini-sweaters have all the humble style of the genuine Weasley sweaters. And they look adorable hanging on their own wire clothes hangers! They're constructed exactly like the real-sized Weasley sweaters, but because of their size, they work up much faster, making these ornaments a great introduction to sweater knitting for the novice knitter. You won't need Molly Weasley's magic needles to knit these for everyone in the family for Christmas!

Back

With color A, CO 14 sts and, beginning with a purl row, work in St st for 21 rows.

Next row (RS): BO 4, k6, BO to end of row—6 sts.

Place rem 6 center back sts on stitch holder or scrap yarn.

Front

With color A, CO 14 sts and, beginning with a purl row, work in St st for 17 rows. Then shape front neck as follows:

Materials for Mini-Weasley Sweater Ornaments

- ☾ Jamieson's *Double Knitting* (100% Shetland wool, 82 yd. [75 m] per 25 g skein), #234 Pine (color A), 1 skein, and #1190 Burnt Umber (color B), 1 skein

- ☾ Or similar yarn that knits to specified gauge: DK-weight wool or wool-blend yarn, about 15 yd. [14 m] of color A and 18" [45.5 cm] of color B

- ☾ US 5 [3.75 mm] needles

- ☾ US 5 [3.75 mm] double-pointed needles, set of 5

- ☾ Stitch markers

- ☾ Stitch holder

- ☾ Tapestry needle

- ☾ About 9" [23 cm] of copper craft wire (18 gauge) for hanger, per hanger

- ☾ Wire cutter and pliers (for hanger)

Gauge

24 sts and 32 rows = 4" [10 cm] in St st using size 5 [3.75 mm] needles

Finished Size

Width: 2" [5 cm]

Length: 2½" [6.5 cm]

Stitch Guide for Mini-Weasley Sweater Ornaments

Stockinette Stitch (St st) Worked in Rows

Row 1 (RS): Knit.

Row 2 (WS): Purl.

Rep rows 1 and 2.

Stockinette Stitch (St st) Worked in Rounds

Knit all sts.

Row 1 (RS): K9, place these same 9 sts onto holder or scrap yarn, k5 rem sts.

Row 2 (WS): P3, p2tog—4 sts.

Row 3: Knit.

Row 4: Purl.

Row 5: BO rem 4 sts.

With RS facing, place first 5 sts from holder back onto needle for other shoulder. (Leave the 4 neck sts on holder.) Join new yarn at edge and work left side of neck as follows:

Row 1 (RS): K3, k2tog—4 sts.

Row 2 (WS): Purl.

Row 3: Knit.

Row 4: BO rem 4 sts.

Cut yarns, leaving 8" [20.5 cm] tails. With tails, sew or graft (see page 160) each shoulder together. Weave in ends.

Sleeves

With stitch marker or scrap yarn, mark edge st 1" [2.5 cm] down from each shoulder seam on front and back.

Pick up 12 sts between markers along left edge. Beginning with a purl row, work in St st for 10 rows. Then work ribbed cuff as follows:

Rows 1 and 3 (WS): P1, *k2, p2; rep from * to last 3 sts, k2, p1.

Row 2 (RS): K1, *p2, k2; rep from * to last 3 sts, p2, k1.

Row 4: BO in patt.

Cut yarn, leaving an 8" [20.5 cm] tail. With tail, sew sleeve and left side seam using mattress st (see page 160) or whipstitch (see page 160). Weave in these ends.

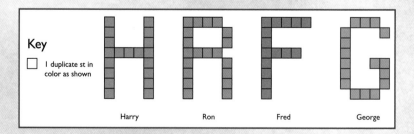

Key

☐ | duplicate st in color as shown

Harry   Ron   Fred   George

Pick up 12 sts between markers along right edge and work second sleeve the same as the first.

Fold cuffs to RS.

Finishing

Neckband

Place 6 back neck sts on one dpn. Join new yarn at right side of back neck and knit across. With second dpn, pick up 4 sts down left side of neck. Place 4 front neck sts on third dpn and knit across. With fourth dpn, pick up 4 sts up right side of neck—18 sts. Work 3 rnds in St st. BO sts loosely. Cut yarn, leaving an 8" [20.5 cm] tail, and weave in all rem ends.

Roll neck edge to RS.

Initial

With color B, work desired initial in duplicate st (see page 157) on sweater front (see chart for initials on page 120).

Hanger

With wire cutter, cut a piece of wire approximately 9" [23 cm] long. Bend wire over knitting needle or finger about 2½" [6.5 cm] from one end. Continuing along wire, bend again about 3" [7.5 cm] further, forming a triangle. Wrap first, shorter end around second, longer end where they cross at the top of the triangle. Trim short end and crimp with pliers so it won't snag the sweater. Bend remaining long end straight,

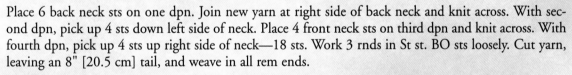

then bend once over knitting needle or finger to form hanger hook. Trim end with wire cutters. Place the sweater on the hanger and hang the hanger from a tree branch.

Materials for Golden Snitch Balls

- Jamieson's *Double Knitting* (100% Shetland wool, 82 yd. [75 m] per 25 g skein), #1190 Burnt Umber, 1 skein
- Or similar yarn that knits to specified gauge. About 3½ yd. [3 m] per Snitch
- US 3 [3.25 mm] double-pointed needles
- Polyester fiberfill or scrap yarn for stuffing
- Tapestry needle
- About 15" [38 cm] clear craft cord [.8 mm], per ornament

Finished Size

Width: 1" [2.5 cm]

Length: 1½" [4 cm]

Note: With a larger gauge yarn, you can make larger Snitch balls or with a finer gauge yarn, you can make even smaller ones.

Gauge

24 sts and 36 rnds = 4" [10 cm] in St st using size 3 [3.25 mm] needles

Golden Snitch Balls

Simple, rustic golden balls you can knit with the leftovers from your mini-Weasleys. Hanging from their own clear wire loops, they appear to fly in the branches. Can your Seeker spot them all?

Instructions

CO 6 sts onto three dpns and join in a circle, being careful not to twist sts.

Rnd 1: *K1f&b, k1; rep from * to end of rnd—9 sts.

Rnd 2: *K1f&b, k2; rep from * to end of rnd—12 sts.

Rnd 3: Knit.

Rnd 4: *K1f&b, k3; rep from * to end of rnd—15 sts.

Rnds 5 and 6: Knit.

Rnd 7: *K1f&b, k4; rep from * to end of rnd—18 sts.

Rnd 8: Knit.

Rnd 9: *K1, k2tog, k3; rep from * to end of rnd—15 sts.

Rnds 10 and 11: Knit.

Rnd 12: *K1, k2tog, k2; rep from * to end of rnd—12 sts.

Rnd 13: Knit.

Stuff Snitch as full as possible at this point with fiberfill or small scraps of yarn.

Rnd 14: *K1, k2tog, k1; rep from * to end of rnd—9 sts.

Rnd 15: *K1, k2tog; rep from * to end of rnd—6 sts.

Finishing

Finish stuffing Snitch to desired fullness. Cut yarn, leaving an 8" [20.5 cm] tail, and thread tail through rem sts to close top of Snitch.

Cut a piece of clear craft cord approximately 15" [38 cm] long and thread through rem sts. Tie knot in cord, trim ends, and pull cord so that ends are hidden in last sts. Thread cord loop and yarn tail together on tapestry needle, insert into bottom of Snitch, and pull up through the center and out the top of Snitch.

Note: Pulling the ends through to the top helps give the bottom a nice rounded shape.

Tie two yarn ends together to form knot, trim ends, and bury knot in body of Snitch. Use the plastic cord loop to hang the Snitch from a tree branch.

Materials

- ☾ Colinette *Isis* (100% viscose; 108 yd. [100 m] per 100 g hank), #071 Fire (yarn A), 1 hank, and Colinette *Silky Chic* (100% nylon; 221 yd. [202 m] per 100 g hank), #071 Fire (yarn B), 1 hank
- ☾ Or similar yarn that knits to specified gauge: ribbon yarn, about 100 yd. [90 m] (yarn A), and furry novelty yarn, about 180 yd. [165 m] (yarn B)
- ☾ US 11 [8 mm] needles
- ☾ 6 large faceted acrylic beads
- ☾ Beading needle or other thin needle with large eye
- ☾ Stitch holder
- ☾ Tapestry needle

Gauge

10 sts and 14 rows = 4" [10 cm] in garter st using size 11 [8 mm] needles with both yarns held together

Finished Size

Width at top: 5½" [14 cm]

Length: 66" [167.5 cm]

PHOENIX TEARS SCARF

Designer – Heather Brack ☾ *Pattern Rating – First Year*

Phoenixes are full of powerful magic: Their tail feathers are used to make wands, and their tears have healing powers. This scarf represents the life of a phoenix, starting in drop-stitch flames, with the magical tail feathers and phoenix tears at the other end. It's knit in a fabulously silky and fiery yarn, as wonderful to knit with as it is to wear. Make one for yourself or share the magic of the phoenix with someone else!

Instructions

Note: Scarf is knit in three sections, beginning with the flames, then the center, and finally the plumage.

Flame Section

With yarn A, CO 15 sts. Knit 1 row.

Work dropped wraps st, as described in stitch guide, for 18" [45.5 cm]. Do not cut yarn.

Center Section

Join yarn B and, holding yarn A and yarn B together, work in garter st for 35" [89 cm].

Cut yarn A, leaving yarn B attached to work.

Plumage

There are two types of plumage on this scarf: three tail feathers and two curly plumes with phoenix tears. Begin with the tail feathers.

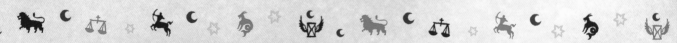

Tail Feathers

Note: You need to work with yarn B held double, so either split the skein into two equal balls, by weight, or wind it into a center-pull ball and use both the inside and outside ends.

Join second strand of yarn B and, holding the two strands of yarn B together, knit first 3 sts for the first tail feather. Place rem 12 sts on stitch holder or scrap yarn. Continue to work same 3 sts in garter st for 13" [33 cm].

> **Next row:** K3tog, cut yarn, leaving an 8" [20.5 cm] tail, and pull tail through last st.

With double strand of yarn B, knit next 9 sts from holder, continuing to hold last 3 sts in reserve. Work in garter st for 9" [23 cm].

> **Row 1:** K2tog, knit to end of row.

Rep row 1 until 1 st rem. Cut yarn, leaving an 8" [20.5 cm] tail, and draw tail through last st.

With double strand of yarn B, work third tail feather over final 3 sts in same manner as first tail feather.

Curly Plumes with Phoenix Tears

Using yarn A, CO 80 sts.

> **Rows 1 and 2:** *K2tog; rep from * across row—40 sts.
> **Rows 3 and 4:** Knit.

BO tightly.

Cut a 10" [25.5 cm] length of yarn A and tie a knot about 3" [7.5 cm] from one end. Slip a bead onto the yarn and down to the knot and then tie another knot so the bead is held firmly in place. *Slip another bead down to the last knot made, then tie another knot to hold the second bead firmly in place; rep from * once more (3 beads total).

Make tassel: Wrap yarn A around the palm of your hand about 6 times (or around a piece of cardboard cut to make loops about 3½" [9 cm] to 4" [10 cm] long). Break yarn, leaving at least an 8" [20.5 cm]

Stitch Guide for This Project

Dropped Wraps St Worked in Rows

Row 1: Knit all sts, wrapping each st twice.

Row 2: Knit all sts, letting the extra wraps drop from the needle.

Rep rows 1 and 2.

Garter Stitch Worked in Rows

Knit all sts.

tail. Use the 3" [7.5 cm] long end of the beaded string to tie the top of the loops, then wrap the 8" [20.5 cm] tail around the strands several times about ½" [1.3 cm] from top of loops to secure the strands and form a tassel. Cut the ends of the tassel and trim them to an even length.

Tie the beaded strand securely to one end of the curly plume: Weave in ends.

Make a second curly plume the same as the first.

Finishing

Sew the curly plumes in the gaps between the straight plumes and weave in all rem ends.

Home at Hogwarts

It may be colder at Durmstrang, but cozy knits are still a winter necessity at Hogwarts! Every young wizard could use some casual sweaters, hats, and mittens for after class or for weekend trips to Hogsmeade. All these patterns were inspired by the extraordinary knits created for the characters' ordinary daywear in the films. There's Harry's traditional red cable sweater, Hermione's hat and mittens from Hogsmeade, Ron's incredible Animal Crackers lion hat, and his latest and greatest initial sweater from home.

The best part: True fans will recognize them as genuine Harry Potter garb, but Muggles will never know!

Materials

- ☾ Jo Sharp *Classic DK Wool* (100% wool, 107 yd. [98 m] per 50 g ball): #309 Cherry, 12 (13, 15, 17) balls

- ☾ Or similar yarn that knits to specified gauge: DK-weight wool or wool-blend yarn, about 1,184 (1,347, 1,681, 1,827) yd. [1,082 (1,231, 1,537, 1,670) m]

- ☾ US 4 [3.25 mm] needles

- ☾ US 4 [3.25 mm] 16" [40 cm] circular needle

- ☾ US 6 [4 mm] needles

- ☾ Stitch holder

- ☾ Tapestry needle

Gauge

30 sts and 29 rows = 4" [10 cm] in cable rib patt using size 6 [4 mm] needles, with rib relaxed

Finished Size

Child M (Child L, Adult S, Adult M, Adult L)

To fit chest: 24 (28, 32, 36, 40)" [61 (71, 81.5, 91.5, 101.5) cm]

Finished chest circumference: 27¼ (31, 34½, 38½, 42)" [69 (78.5, 87.5, 98, 106.5) cm], with cable rib relaxed

Length: 18 (22, 24½, 25½, 26½)" [45.5 (56, 62, 65, 67.5) cm]

Sample shown: Size Child L

HARRY'S RED CABLE SWEATER

Designer - Alison Hansel ☾ *Pattern Rating - Ordinary Wizarding Level*

What every young wizard wears to battle You-Know-Who! Just like the sweater Harry wore in *The Sorcerer's Stone*, this classic rib and cable pattern, knit in a wonderful classic wool, is a class act through and through. Although the cable rib pattern requires some attention, the overall sweater shaping is rather simple—with modified drop shoulders and standard shaping at neck and shoulders—making this sweater a great project for intermediate wizards preparing for their O.W.L.s. Knit it for your young lad to wear to class or for yourself to wear the next time you have to get past Fluffy and through the trap door!

Back

With smaller needles, CO 102 (116, 130, 144, 158) sts.

Work in single rib, as described in the stitch guide, until piece measures 2 (2, 2, 2½, 2½)" [5 (5, 5, 6.5, 6.5) cm] from CO edge, ending with a WS row completed.

Switch to larger needles and work in cable rib patt, as described in the stitch guide, until back measures 11 (14, 15½, 16, 16½)" [28 (35.5, 39, 40.5, 42) cm] from CO edge or desired length to armholes.

Armhole Shaping

Maintaining cable rib patt, BO 4 sts beg next 2 rows—94 (108, 122, 136, 150) sts.

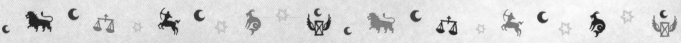

Continue in cable rib patt until armhole measures 6½ (7½, 8½, 9, 9½)" [16.5, 19, 21.5, 23, 24) cm], ending with a WS row completed.

Note: The back left neck and shoulder are shaped first, and then the right.

Back Left Shoulder and Neck Shaping

Next row (RS): BO 8 (8, 8, 10, 12) sts, work in patt until you have 28 (30, 34, 38, 42) sts on right needle, turn.

At this point, leave the rem 58 (70, 80, 88, 96) sts on the other needle, working only the back left sts, as follows:

Row 1 (WS): BO 8 sts, work in patt to end of row—20 (22, 26, 30, 34) sts.

Row 2: BO 8 (8, 8, 10, 12) sts, work in patt to end of row—12 (14, 18, 20, 22) sts.

Row 3: BO 2 sts, work in patt to end of row—10 (12, 16, 18, 20) sts.

Row 4: BO 6 (6, 8, 10, 10) sts, work in patt to end of row—4 (6, 8, 8, 10) sts.

Row 5: Work in patt.

BO rem 4 (6, 8, 8, 10) sts.

Back Right Shoulder and Neck Shaping

Rejoin yarn to right edge of neck and shape right shoulder and neck as follows:

Row 1 (RS): BO center 22 (32, 38, 40, 42) sts, work in patt to end of row—36 (38, 42, 48, 54) sts.

Row 2 (WS): BO 8 (8, 8, 10, 12) sts, work in patt to end of row—28 (30, 34, 38, 42) sts.

Row 3: BO 8 sts, work in patt to end of row—20 (22, 26, 30, 34) sts.

Row 4: BO 8 (8, 8, 10, 12) sts, work in patt to end of row—12 (14, 18, 20, 22) sts.

Row 5: BO 2 sts, work in patt to end of row—10 (12, 16, 18, 20) sts.

Row 6: BO 6 (6, 8, 10, 10) sts, work in patt to end of row—4 (6, 8, 8, 10) sts.

Row 7: Work in patt.

BO rem 4 (6, 8, 8, 10) sts.

Stitch Guide for This Project

Single Rib (1x1 Rib) Worked in Rows or Rounds over Even Number of Sts

Row/Rnd 1: *K1, p1; rep from * to end of row/rnd.

Rep row/rnd 1.

Cable Rib Pattern

Rows 1, 3, and 5 (RS): *K4, p2, K6, p2; rep from * to last 4 sts, k4.

Rows 2, 4, 6, and 8 (WS): P4, *k2, p6, k2, p4; rep from * to end of row.

Row 7: *K4, p2, c6f, p2; rep from * to last 4 sts, k4.

Rep rows 1–8.

Special Technique for This Project

c6f (Cable 6 Front)

Sl next 3 sts onto cable needle and hold at front of work. K3 from left needle, then k3 from cable needle.

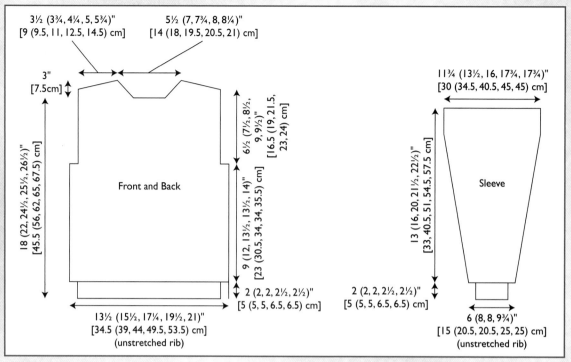

Front and Back

3½ (3¾, 4¼, 5, 5¾)" [9 (9.5, 11, 12.5, 14.5) cm]

5½ (7, 7¾, 8, 8½)" [14 (18, 19.5, 20.5, 21) cm]

3" [7.5cm]

18 (22, 24½, 25½, 26½)" [45.5 (56, 62, 65, 67.5) cm]

6½ (7½, 8½, 9, 9½)" [16.5 (19, 21.5, 23, 24) cm]

9 (12, 13½, 13½, 14)" [23 (30.5, 34, 34, 35.5) cm]

2 (2, 2, 2½, 2½)" [5 (5, 5, 6.5, 6.5) cm]

13½ (15½, 17¼, 19½, 21)" [34.5 (39, 44, 49.5, 53.5) cm] (unstretched rib)

Sleeve

11¾ (13½, 16, 17¾, 17¾)" [30 (34.5, 40.5, 45, 45) cm]

13 (16, 20, 21½, 22½)" [33 (40.5, 51, 54.5, 57.5) cm]

2 (2, 2, 2½, 2½)" [5 (5, 5, 6.5, 6.5) cm]

6 (8, 8, 9¾)" [15 (20.5, 20.5, 25, 25) cm] (unstretched rib)

Front

Work as for back until armhole measures 4½ (5½, 6½, 7, 7½)" [10, 14, 16.5, 18, 19) cm], ending with a WS row completed.

Note: The left front neck and shoulder are shaped first, and then the right.

Front Left Shoulder and Neck Shaping

Next row (RS): Work 40 (42, 46, 52, 58) sts in patt, turn.

At this point, leave the rem 54 (66, 76, 84, 92) sts on the other needle, working only the front left sts, as follows:

Note: Working the decreases at the neck edge in rev St st provides a clean line dividing the cable pattern sts from the neckline.

Row 1 (WS): BO 4 sts, work in patt to end of row—36 (38, 42, 48, 54) sts.

Row 2: Work in patt to last 3 sts, p2tog, p1—35 (37, 41, 47, 53) sts.

Row 3: K1, k2tog, work in patt to end of row—34 (36, 40, 46, 52) sts.

Row 4: Rep row 2—33 (35, 39, 45, 51) sts.

Row 5: Work in patt.

Rep last 2 rows 5 times more—28 (30, 34, 40, 46) sts rem. Armhole should measure about 6½ (7½, 8½, 9, 9½)" [16.5, 19, 21.5, 23, 24) cm].

Continue neck decreases and *at the same time* begin shoulder decreases, as follows:

Row 1 (RS): BO 8 (8, 8, 10, 12) sts, work to last 3 sts, p2tog, p1—19 (21, 25, 29, 33) sts.

Row 2 and all other WS rows: Work in patt.

Row 3: BO 8 (8, 8, 10, 12) sts, work to last 3 sts, p2tog, p1—10 (12, 16, 18, 20) sts.

Row 5: BO 6 (6, 8, 10, 10) sts, work in patt to end of row—4 (6, 8, 8, 10) sts.

Row 7: BO rem 4 (6, 8, 8, 10) sts.

Front Right Shoulder and Neck Shaping

Rejoin yarn at right edge of neck and shape right shoulder and neck as follows:

Row 1 (RS): BO center 14 (24, 30, 32, 34) sts, work in patt to end of row—40 (42, 46, 52, 58) sts.

Row 2 (WS): Work in patt.

Row 3: BO 4 sts, work in patt to end of row—36 (38, 42, 48, 54) sts.

Row 4: Work in patt to last 3 sts, ssk, k1—35 (37, 41, 47, 53) sts.

Row 5: P1, ssp, work in patt to end of row—34 (36, 40, 46, 52) sts.

Row 6: Rep row 4—33 (35, 39, 45, 51) sts.

Row 7: Work in patt.

Rep last 2 rows 5 times more—28 (30, 34, 40, 46) sts. Armhole should measure about 6½ (7½, 8½, 9, 9½)" [16.5, 19, 21.5, 23, 24) cm].

Continue neck decreases and *at the same time* begin shoulder decreases, as follows:

Row 1 (WS): BO 8 (8, 8, 10, 12) sts, work to last 3 sts, k2tog, k1—19 (21, 25, 29, 33) sts.

Row 2 and all other RS rows: Work in patt.

Row 3: BO 8 (8, 8, 10, 12) sts, work to last 3 sts, k2tog, k1—10 (12, 16, 18, 20) sts.

Row 5: BO 6 (6, 8, 10, 10) sts, work in patt to end of row—4 (6, 8, 8, 10) sts.

Row 7: BO rem 4 (6, 8, 8, 10) sts.

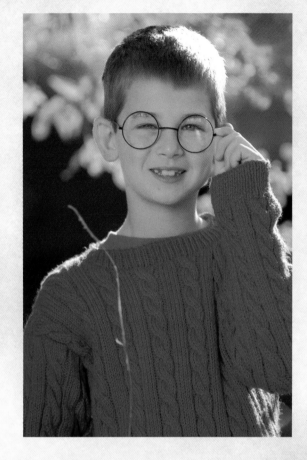

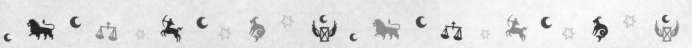

Sleeves

With smaller needles, CO 46 (60, 60, 74, 74) sts and work in single rib for 2 (2, 2, 2½, 2½)" [5 (5, 5, 6.5, 6.5) cm], ending with a WS row completed.

Switch to larger needles and work first 6 rows of cable rib patt.

Begin sleeve increases:

Note: Increasing 1 st in from the edge while keeping the first and last sts in St st maintains an even edge along the sleeve for easier seaming. When incorporating new sts into cable rib patt, do not count these first and last knit sts as part of the pattern.

Row 1 (RS): K1f&b, work in patt to last 2 sts, k1f&b, k1—48 (62, 62, 76, 76) sts.

Rows 2 and 4 (WS): P5, work in patt to last 5 sts, p5.

Row 3: k5, work in patt to last 5 sts, K5.

Row 5: K1f&b, work in patt to last 2 sts, k1f&b, k1—50 (64, 64, 78, 78) sts.

Rows 6 and 8: P1, k1, work in patt to last 2 sts, k1, p1.

Row 7: K1, p1, work in patt to last 2 sts, p1, k1.

Row 9: K1f&b, p1, work in patt to last 2 sts, p1f&b, k1—52 (66, 66, 80, 80) sts.

Row 10 and 12: P1, k2, work in patt to last 3 sts, k2, p1.

Row 11: K1, p2, work in patt to last 3 sts, p2, k1.

Continue to increase in this manner, 1 st in from the edge, every 4th row 18 (18, 27, 27, 27) times more—88 (102, 120, 134, 134) sts.

Work even in patt until sleeve measures 15 (18, 22, 24, 25)" [38 (45.5, 56, 61, 63.5) cm] from CO edge or desired sleeve length. BO all sts in patt.

Make second sleeve the same.

Neckband

Block all pieces to size, according to yarn manufacturer's instructions.

Graft shoulder seams together (see page 160).

Join new yarn at right edge of back neck and with circ needle, pick up and k42 (54, 58, 60, 62) sts across back neck, 18 sts down left side of neck, 14 (24, 30, 32, 34) sts from front neck, and 18 sts up right side of neck—92 (114, 124, 128, 132) sts around neckline. Join in a circle and work in single rib for 8 rnds. BO all sts loosely in patt.

Finishing

Sew side and sleeve seams, using mattress stitch (see page 160), and weave in all ends.

Lightly steam seams to smooth out any puckers, if necessary.

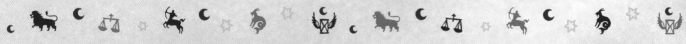

HERMIONE'S CABLE AND BOBBLE HAT

Designer – Lauren Kent
Pattern Rating – Ordinary Wizarding Level

Knit this Aran-style cabled hat, modeled after the one Hermione wore to Hogsmeade in *Prisoner of Azkaban*, for your next visit to Britain's only wizarding village. The cabling is thoroughly addictive; ambitious knitters may finish this hat in a single weekend! The alpaca/silk/merino yarn is soft and a tiny bit fuzzy against your forehead. It's perfect for snowball fights, long wintertime walks, or as the final touch on your Hermione costume.

Instructions

Brim

CO 96 sts onto circular needle. Pm to note beg rnd and join in a circle, being careful not to twist sts.

Rnds 1–30: Work in double rib, as described in the stitch guide.

Hat Body

For rnds 31–65, follow the chart on page 135 or instructions below. For all rnds, rep patt 3 times per rnd.

Rnd 31: *K6, p15, k2, p1, k6, p2; rep from * to end of rnd.
Rnd 32: *K6, p13, c2rp2, p1, k6, p2; rep from * to end of rnd.
Rnd 33: *K6, p13, k2, p3, k6, p2; rep from * to end of rnd.
Rnd 34: *C6f, p11, c2rp2, p3, c6f, p2; rep from * to end of rnd.
Rnd 35: *K6, p11, k2, p5, k6, p2; rep from * to end of rnd.

Materials

- Knit Picks *Andean Silk* (55% superfine alpaca, 23% silk, 22% merino wool; 96 yd. [88 m] per 50 g ball), #23781 Cranberry, 2 balls
- Or similar yarn that knits to specified gauge: worsted-weight wool or wool-blend yarn, about 180 yd. [165 m]
- US 7 [4.5 mm] 16" [40 cm] circular needle
- US 7 [4.5 mm] double-pointed needles
- Cable needle
- Stitch markers
- Tapestry needle

Gauge

21 sts and 31 rnds = 4" [10 cm] in St st using size 7 [4.5 mm] needles

Finished Size

Circumference: 20" [51 cm]

Circumference at brim: 17" [43 cm] in unstretched rib

Height: 9" [23 cm] with cuffed brim

Note: Measurements can be increased or decreased by blocking more or less vigorously.

Stitch Guide for This Project

Double Rib (2x2 Rib) Worked in Rounds

Rnd 1: *K2, p2; rep from * to end of rnd.

Rep rnd 1.

Special Techniques for This Project

c6f (Cable 6 Front)

Sl next 3 sts onto cable needle and hold at front of work. K3 from left needle, then k3 from cable needle.

c2rp2 (Cable 2 Right, Purl 2)

Sl next 2 sts onto cable needle and hold at back of work. K2 from left needle, then p2 from cable needle.

mb (Make Bobble)

1. [K, p, k] into next st.
2. Turn work, p3.
3. Turn, k3.
4. Turn, p3.
5. Turn, pass 2nd and 3rd sts over 1st st, then knit into the back of that st.

c2lp2 (Cable 2 Left, Purl 2)

Sl next 2 sts onto cable needle and hold at front of work. P2 from left needle, then k2 from cable needle.

c4f (Cable 4 Front)

Sl next 2 sts onto cable needle and hold at front of work. K2 from left needle, then k2 sts from cable needle.

c2f (Cable 2 Front)

Sl next st onto cable needle and hold at front of work. K1 from left needle, then k1 from cable needle.

c1lp1 (Cable 1 Left, Purl 1)

Sl next st onto cable needle and hold at front of work. P1 from left needle, then k1 from cable needle.

Rnd 36: *K6, p9, c2rp2, p5, k6, p2; rep from * to end of rnd.

Rnd 37: *K6, p9, k2, p7, k6, p2; rep from * to end of rnd.

Rnd 38: *C6f, p7, c2rp2, p7, c6f, p2; rep from * to end of rnd.

Rnd 39: *K6, p7, k2, p9, k6, p2; rep from * to end of rnd.

Rnd 40: *K6, p5, c2rp2, p9, k6, p2; rep from * to end of rnd.

Rnd 41: *K6, p5, k2, p11, k6, p2; rep from * to end of rnd.

Rnd 42: *C6f, p3, c2rp2, p11, c6f, p2; rep from * to end of rnd.

Rnd 43: *K6, p3, k2, p13, k6, p2; rep from * to end of rnd.

Rnd 44: *K6, p1, c2rp2, p13, k6, p2; rep from * to end of rnd.

Rnd 45: *K6, p1, k2, p15, k6, p2; rep from * to end of rnd.

Rnd 46: *C6f, p1, k2, p7, mb, p7, c6f, p2; rep from * to end of rnd.

Rnd 47: *K6, p1, k2, p15, k6, p2; rep from * to end of rnd.

Rnd 48: *K6, p1, c2lp2, p13, k6, p2; rep from * to end of rnd.

Rnd 49: *K6, p3, k2, p13, k6, p2; rep from * to end of rnd.

Rnd 50: *C6f, p3, c2lp2, p11, c6f, p2; rep from * to end of rnd.

Rnd 51: *K6, p5, k2, p11, k6, p2; rep from * to end of rnd.

Rnd 52: *K6, p5, c2lp2, p9, k6, p2; rep from * to end of rnd.

Rnd 53: *K6, p7, k2, p9, k6, p2; rep from * to end of rnd.

Rnd 54: *C6f, p7, c2lp2, p7, c6f, p2; rep from * to end of rnd.

Rnd 55: *K6, p9, k2, p7, k6, p2; rep from * to end of rnd.

Rnd 56: *K6, p9, c2lp2, p5, k6, p2; rep from * to end of rnd.

Rnd 57: *K6, p11, k2, p5, k6, p2; rep from * to end of rnd.

Rnd 58: *C6f, p11, c2lp2, p3, c6f, p2; rep from * to end of rnd.

Rnd 59: *K6, p13, k2, p3, k6, p2; rep from * to end of rnd.

Rnd 60: *K6, p13, c2lp2, p1, k6, p2; rep from * to end of rnd.

Rnd 61: *K6, p15, k2, p1, k6, p2; rep from * to end of rnd.

Rnd 62: *C6f, p7, mb, p7, k2, p1, c6f, p2; rep from * to end of rnd.

Rnd 63: *K6, p15, k2, p1, k6, p2; rep from * to end of rnd.

Rnd 64: *K6, p13, c2rp2, p1, k6, p2; rep from * to end of rnd.

Rnd 65: *K6, p13, k2, p3, k6, p2; rep from * to end of rnd.

Key

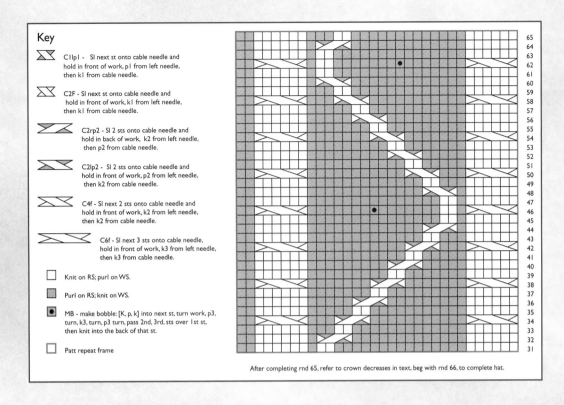

C1lp1 - Sl next st onto cable needle and hold in front of work, p1 from left needle, then k1 from cable needle.

C2F - Sl next st onto cable needle and hold in front of work, k1 from left needle, then k1 from cable needle.

C2rp2 - Sl 2 sts onto cable needle and hold in back of work, k2 from left needle, then p2 from cable needle.

C2lp2 - Sl 2 sts onto cable needle and hold in front of work, p2 from left needle, then k2 from cable needle.

C4f - Sl next 2 sts onto cable needle and hold in front of work, k2 from left needle, then k2 from cable needle.

C6f - Sl next 3 sts onto cable needle, hold in front of work, k3 from left needle, then k3 from cable needle.

☐ Knit on RS; purl on WS.

▨ Purl on RS; knit on WS.

⊙ MB - make bobble: [K, p, k] into next st, turn work, p3, turn, k3, turn, p3 turn, pass 2nd, 3rd, sts over 1st st, then knit into the back of that st.

☐ Patt repeat frame

After completing rnd 65, refer to crown decreases in text, beg with rnd 66, to complete hat.

Crown

To decrease for the crown, follow the instructions here, continuing to rep patt 3 times per rnd. When sts no longer fit on circ needle, switch to dpns.

Rnd 66: *C6f, p2, p2tog, p3, p2tog, p2, c2rp2, p3, c6f, p2; rep from * to end of rnd—90 sts.

Rnd 67: *K6, p9, k2, p5, k6, p2; rep from * to end of rnd.

Rnd 68: *K6, p7, c2rp2, p5, k6, p2; rep from * to end of rnd.

Rnd 69: *K6, p7, k2, p7, k6, p2; rep from * to end of rnd.

Rnd 70: *C6f, p2, p2tog, p1, c2rp2, p2, p2tog, p3, c6f, p2; rep from * to end of rnd—84 sts.

Rnd 71: *K6, p4, k2, p8, k6, p2; rep from * to end of rnd.

Rnd 72: *K6, p2, c2rp2, p8, k6, p2; rep from * to end of rnd.

Rnd 73: *K6, p2, k2, p10, k6, p2; rep from * to end of rnd.

Rnd 74: *C6f, p2tog, k2, p4, mb, p2, p2tog, p1, c6f, p2tog; rep from * to end of rnd—75 sts.

Rnd 75: *K6, p1, k2, p9, k6, p1; rep from * to end of rnd.

Rnd 76: *K1, ssk, k2tog, k1, p1, c2lp2, p7, k1, ssk, k2tog, k1, p1; rep from * to end of rnd—63 sts.

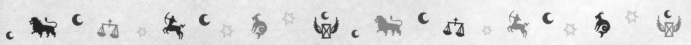

Rnd 77: *K4, p1, p2tog, k2, p1, p2tog, p1, p2tog, p1, k4, p1; rep from * to end of rnd— 54 sts.

Rnd 78: *C4f, p2, c2lp2, p3, c4f, p1; rep from * to end of rnd.

Rnd 79: *[K2tog] 2 times, [p2tog] 2 times, k2tog, p2tog, p1, [k2tog] 2 times, p1; rep from * to end of rnd—30 sts.

Rnd 80: *C2f, p2, c1lp1, p1, c2f, p1; rep from * to end of rnd.

Rnd 81: *K2tog, p2tog, k2tog, p2tog, k2tog; rep from * to end of rnd— 15 sts.

Cut yarn, leaving an 8" [20.5 cm] tail. Thread tail through rem sts to close top of hat.

Finishing

Weave in ends.

Note: Blocking the hat will help to settle and even out the cables as well as allow you to stretch it to fit a larger head.

To block the hat, wash it according to the yarn manufacturer's instructions and press it in a towel to remove excess water. If you have something round that's slightly smaller than a human head—a large bowl, ball, or balloon, for example—put the hat on the object, being careful not to stretch it out of shape, and let it dry. Otherwise, fold the hat closed and pin to a blocking board or folded towel so that the stitches are opened but not stretched tight. When the hat is dry, remove it from the blocking surface, fold up the brim, and wear!

HERMIONE'S CABLE AND BOBBLE MITTENS

Designer – Lauren Kent ☾
Pattern Rating – Ordinary Wizarding Level

Created to match Hermione's Cable and Bobble Hat seen in *Prisoner of Azkaban*, these mittens will keep your hands toasty all winter, whether you wear them with the hat, with a house scarf, or on their own. The zigzag cable, bordered by delicate 2-stitch ropes, is fun and deceptively easy to knit, while the mitten styling adds a bit of a challenge. The alpaca/silk/merino blend yarn is wonderfully soft with a bit of sheen to show off the stitch work, and it's just the right shade of red. These would make a terrific winter birthday present for the Hermione in your life, or keep them for yourself—we won't tell!

Instructions

If you like a particularly snug cuff, work the ribbing on US 5 [3.75 mm] needles, then switch to US 6 [4 mm] at the start of the cabling.

Left Mitten

CO 40 sts onto four dpns and join in a circle, being careful not to twist sts.

Note: This project refers to the dpns by number throughout the pattern, with needle 1 being the first one worked in each rnd. It is based on having a set of five dpns (four needles holding sts and one used to knit). If your needle set contains only four dpns, place the sts assigned to needles 1 and 2 on a single needle, with a stitch marker between them.

Rnds 1–17: Work in knit-first double rib, as described in the stitch guide (see page 138).

Rnds 18–24: Needles 1 and 2: work 20-st left-hand cable patt (see chart on page 140 or instructions on page 141), beg with rnd 1; needles 3 and 4: k20.

Materials

- ☾ Knit Picks *Andean Silk* (55% superfine alpaca, 23% silk, 22% merino wool; 96 yd. [88 m] per 50 g ball), #23781 Cranberry, 2 skeins

- ☾ Or similar yarn that knits to specified gauge: worsted-weight wool or wool-blend yarn, about 175 yd. [160 m]

- ☾ US 6 [4 mm] double-pointed needles, set of 5

- ☾ US 5 [3.75 mm] double-pointed needles (optional)

- ☾ Cable needle

- ☾ Stitch markers

- ☾ Tapestry needle

Gauge

22 sts and 31 rnds = 4" [10 cm] in St st using size 6 [4 mm] needles

Finished Size

Circumference at palm: 6½" [16.5 cm]

Circumference at wrist: 5½" [14 cm] in unstretched rib

Length: 11½" [29 cm] uncuffed

Note: The extensive cabling makes it somewhat difficult to resize these mittens for much larger or smaller hands. If you want to work them to a different size, try blocking to size or working with larger or smaller needles or heavier- or lighter-weight yarn.

Stitch Guide for This Project

Knit-First Double Rib (2x2 Rib) Worked in Rounds

Rnd 1: *K2, p2; rep from * to end of rnd.

Rep rnd 1.

Purl-First Double Rib (2x2 Rib) Worked in Rounds

Rnd 1: *P2, k2; rep from * to end of rnd.

Rep rnd 1.

Stockinette Stitch (St st) Worked in Rnds

Knit all sts.

Special Techniques for This Project

c2b (Cable 2 Back)

Sl next st onto cable needle and hold in back of work. K1 from left needle, then k1 from cable needle.

c2rp2 (Cable 2 Right, Purl 2)

Sl next 2 sts onto cable needle and hold in back of work. K2 from left needle, then p2 from cable needle.

mb (Make Bobble)

1. [K, p, k] into next st.
2. Turn work, p3.
3. Turn, k3.
4. Turn, p3.
5. Turn, pass 2nd and 3rd sts over 1st st, then knit into the back of that st.

Note: Unless noted otherwise, continue working left-hand cable patt. The cable row that corresponds with each mitten rnd is mentioned only when needed for clarity.

Increase for Thumb Gusset

Rnd 25: Needles 1 and 2: work cable rnd 8; needles 3 and 4: k18, pm, k1, k1b into prev st, k1—41 sts.

Rnd 26: Needles 1 and 2: work next rnd of left-hand cable patt; needles 3 and 4: knit across all sts.

Rnd 27: Needles 1 and 2: work next rnd of left-hand cable patt; needles 3 and 4: k18, slip marker, k1, k1b into prev st, knit to end of rnd—42 sts.

Rep rnds 26 and 27 for the next 21 rnds—52 sts rem.

Rnd 49: Needles 1 and 2: work rnd 8 of cable patt; needles 3 and 4: k32.

Thread tapestry needle with a strand of scrap yarn about 18" [45.5 cm] long and slip 38 sts—from needles 1, 2, 3, and the first 8 sts of needle 4 (up to the marker)—onto the scrap yarn. CO 2 sts, using backward loop cast-on. Divide these 2 sts and the rem 14 thumb sts onto three dpns and join in a circle, being careful not to twist sts.

Left Thumb

Rnds 1–14: Knit.

Rnd 15: *K2tog; rep from * to end of rnd—8 sts.

Rnd 16: Rep rnd 15—4 sts.

Cut yarn, leaving an 8" [20.5 cm] tail. Thread tail through rem sts to close top of thumb.

Left Palm and Finger Area

Slip 38 held sts from scrap yarn back onto needles (10 sts each on needles 1, 2, and 3; 8 sts on needle 4). Join yarn at needle 1, being careful not to twist sts.

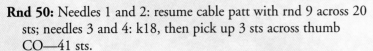

Rnd 50: Needles 1 and 2: resume cable patt with rnd 9 across 20 sts; needles 3 and 4: k18, then pick up 3 sts across thumb CO—41 sts.

Rnd 51: With needle 1, pick up 1 more st across thumb CO, then work cable patt rnd 10 across needles 1 and 2; needles 3 and 4: k17, ssk, k2—41 sts.

Rnd 52: On needle 1, p2tog (picked-up st and first st of cable patt), work remainder of cable patt rnd 11 (beginning with k2) across needles 1 and 2; needles 3 and 4: k20—40 sts.

Rnds 53–77: Needles 1 and 2: work next cable patt rnd across 20 sts; needles 3 and 4: k20.

Rnd 78: Needles 1 and 2: work cable patt rnd 13; needles 3 and 4, k20.

Decrease for Fingertip Area

Rnd 79: P1, c2b, p2, p2tog, p1, p2tog, c2lp2, p1, p2tog, c2b, p1, k4, k2tog, k3, k2tog, k3, k2tog, k4—34 sts.

Rnd 80: P1, k2, p7, k2, p2, k2, p1, k17.

Rnd 81: P1, c2b, p1, p2tog, mb, p2tog, p1, k2, p2tog, c2b, p1, k3, k2tog, k3, k2tog, k2, k2tog, k3—28 sts.

Rnd 82: P1, k2, p5, k2tog, p1, k2, p1, k14—27 sts.

Rnd 83: P1, k2tog, [p2tog] 2 times, c1rp1, p1, k2tog, p1, [k2tog, k1] 4 times, k2tog—18 sts.

Rnd 84: P1, k1, p2, k1, p2, k1, p1, k9.

Rnd 85: K2tog, p2tog, k1, p2tog, ssk, k2tog, k2, k2tog, k1, k2tog—11 sts.

Cut yarn, leaving an 8" [20.5 cm] tail. Thread tail through rem sts to close top of mitten.

Right Mitten

CO 40 sts onto four dpns and join in a circle, being careful not to twist sts.

Rnds 1–17: Work in purl-first double rib, as described in the stitch guide.

Rnds 18–24: On needles 1 and 2: work right-hand 20-st cable patt, beg with rnd 1; needles 3 and 4: k20.

c2lp2 (Cable 2 Left, Purl 2)

Sl next 2 sts onto cable needle and hold in front of work. P2 from left needle, then k2 from cable needle.

c2f (Cable 2 Front)

Sl next st onto cable needle and hold in front of work. K1 from left needle, then k1 from cable needle.

k1b (Lifted Increase) into Prev St

With the previous st on the right needle, insert the left needle into the purl bump 2 rows below the stitch on the needle and knit the st.

c1rp1 (Cable 1 Right, Purl 1)

Sl next st onto cable needle and hold in back of work. K1 from left needle, then p1 from cable needle.

k1b (Lifted Increase) into Next St

Roll the left needle forward, toward you, exposing the purl sts. Insert the right needle tip from top to bottom into the first purl bump on left needle and knit; the active st (still on left needle) is counted as the next st in the following instructions.

c1lp1 (Cable 1 Left, Purl 1)

Sl next st onto cable needle and hold at front of work. P1 from left needle, then K1 from cable needle.

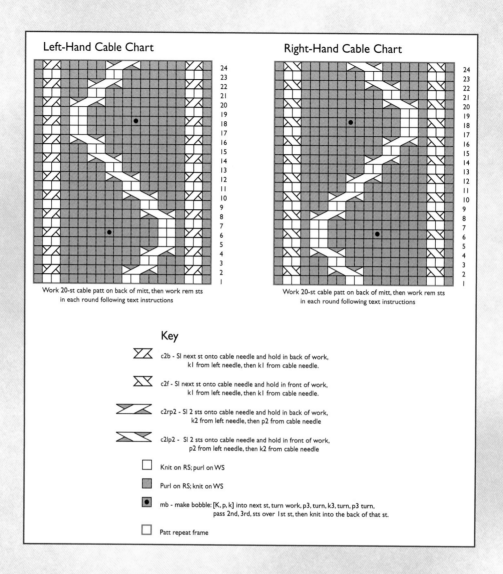

Left-Hand Cable Chart

Right-Hand Cable Chart

Work 20-st cable patt on back of mitt, then work rem sts
in each round following text instructions

Work 20-st cable patt on back of mitt, then work rem sts
in each round following text instructions

Key

c2b - Sl next st onto cable needle and hold in back of work,
k1 from left needle, then k1 from cable needle.

c2f - Sl next st onto cable needle and hold in front of work,
k1 from left needle, then k1 from cable needle.

c2rp2 - Sl 2 sts onto cable needle and hold in back of work,
k2 from left needle, then p2 from cable needle

c2lp2 - Sl 2 sts onto cable needle and hold in front of work,
p2 from left needle, then k2 from cable needle

☐ Knit on RS; purl on WS

▨ Purl on RS; knit on WS

⊡ mb - make bobble: [K, p, k] into next st, turn work, p3, turn, k3, turn, p3 turn,
pass 2nd, 3rd, sts over 1st st, then knit into the back of that st.

☐ Patt repeat frame

Note: Unless noted otherwise, continue working right-hand cable patt. The cable row that corresponds with each mitten rnd is mentioned only when needed for clarity.

Increase for Thumb Gusset

Rnd 25: Needles 1 and 2: work cable rnd 8; needles 3 and 4: k1, k1b into next st, pm, k1, k18—
41 sts.

Rnd 26: Needles 1 and 2: work next rnd of right-hand cable pattern; needles 3 and 4: knit.

Rnd 27: Needles 1 and 2: work next rnd of right-hand cable pattern; needles 3 and 4: knit to 1 st before marker, k1b into next st, slip marker, knit to end of rnd—42 sts.

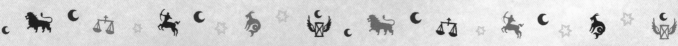

Left-Hand Cable
(Worked Across 20 Sts)

Rnd 1: P1, k2, p5, k2, p7, k2, p1.
Rnd 2: P1, c2b, p3, c2rp2, p7, c2b, p1.
Rnd 3: P1, k2, p3, k2, p9, k2, p1.
Rnd 4: P1, c2b, p1, c2rp2, p9, c2b, p1.
Rnd 5: P1, k2, p1, k2, p11, k2, p1.
Rnd 6: P1, c2b, p1, k2, p5, mb, p5, c2b, p1.
Rnd 7: P1, k2, p1, k2, p11, k2, p1.
Rnd 8: P1, c2b, p1, c2lp2, p9, c2b, p1.
Rnd 9: P1, k2, p3, k2, p9, k2, p1.
Rnd 10: P1, c2b, p3, c2lp2, p7, c2b, p1.
Rnd 11: P1, k2, p5, k2, p7, k2, p1.
Rnd 12: P1, c2b, p5, c2lp2, p5, c2b, p1.
Rnd 13: P1, k2, p7, k2, p5, k2, p1.
Rnd 14: P1, c2b, p7, c2lp2, p3, c2b, p1.
Rnd 15: P1, k2, p9, k2, p3, k2, p1.
Rnd 16: P1, c2b, p9, c2lp2, p1, c2b, p1.
Rnd 17: P1, k2, p11, k2, p1, k2, p1.
Rnd 18: P1, c2b, p5, mb, p5, k2, p1, c2b, p1.
Rnd 19: P1, k2, p11, k2, p1, k2, p1.
Rnd 20: P1, c2b, p9, c2rp2, p1, c2b, p1.
Rnd 21: P1, k2, p9, k2, p3, k2, p1.
Rnd 22: P1, c2b, p7, c2rp2, p3, c2b, p1.
Rnd 23: P1, k2, p7, k2, p5, k2, p1.
Rnd 24: P1, c2b, p5, c2rp2, p5, c2b, p1.
Rep rnds 1–24.

Right-Hand Cable
(Worked Across 20 Sts)

Rnd 1: P1, k2, p7, k2, p5, k2, p1.
Rnd 2: P1, c2f, p7, c2lp2, p3, c2f, p1.
Rnd 3: P1, k2, p9, k2, p3, k2, p1.
Rnd 4: P1, c2f, p9, c2lp2, p1, c2f, p1.
Rnd 5: P1, k2, p11, k2, p1, k2, p1.
Rnd 6: P1, c2f, p5, mb, p5, k2, p1, c2f, p1.
Rnd 7: P1, k2, p11, k2, p1, k2, p1.
Rnd 8: P1, c2f, p9, c2rp2, p1, c2f, p1.
Rnd 9: P1, k2, p9, k2, p3, k2, p1.
Rnd 10: P1, c2f, p7, c2rp2, p3, c2f, p1.
Rnd 11: P1, k2, p7, k2, p5, k2, p1.
Rnd 12: P1, c2f, p5, c2rp2, p5, c2f, p1.
Rnd 13: P1, k2, p5, k2, p7, k2, p1.
Rnd 14: P1, c2f, p3, c2rp2, p7, c2f, p1.
Rnd 15: P1, k2, p3, k2, p9, k2, p1.
Rnd 16: P1, c2f, p1, c2rp2, p9, c2f, p1.
Rnd 17: P1, k2, p1, k2, p11, k2, p1.
Rnd 18: P1, c2f, p1, k2, p5, mb, p5, c2f, p1.
Rnd 19: P1, k2, p1, k2, p11, k2, p1.
Rnd 20: P1, c2f, p1, c2lp2, p9, c2f, p1.
Rnd 21: P1, k2, p3, k2, p9, k2, p1.
Rnd 22: P1, c2f, p3, c2lp2, p7, c2f, p1.
Rnd 23: P1, k2, p5, k2, p7, k2, p1.
Rnd 24: P1, c2f, p5, c2lp2, p5, c2f, p1.
Rep rnds 1–24.

Rep rnds 26 and 27 for the next 21 rnds—52 sts rem.

Rnd 49: Needles 1 and 2: work right-hand cable patt rnd 8; needle 3: k14 (up to marker).

Thread tapestry needle with a strand of scrap yarn about 18" [45.5 cm] long and slip unworked sts from needle 3, along with all sts from needles 1, 2, and 4, onto scrap yarn using tapestry needle—14 sts rem. CO 2 sts at the end of needle 3 using backward loop cast-on. Divide these 16 sts evenly across three needles and join in a circle, being careful not to twist sts.

Right Thumb

Rnds 1–14: Knit.

Rnd 15: *K2tog; rep from * to end of rnd—8 sts.

Rnd 16: Rep rnd 15—4 sts.

Cut yarn, leaving an 8" [20.5 cm] tail. Thread tail through rem sts to close top of thumb.

Right Palm and Finger Area

Slip 38 held sts from scrap yarn back onto needles (8 sts on needle 3 and 10 sts each on needles 1, 2, and 4). Join yarn at palm side of thumb gusset (needle 3), being careful not to twist sts.

Note: The dpns are renumbered for the remainder of the project. The needle where yarn has been joined (previously needle 3) is now needle 1. Other needles are renumbered in order, so that the cable patt is now worked across needles 3 and 4.

Rnd 50: Needles 1 and 2: k18; needles 3 and 4: resume cable patt with rnd 9 across 20 sts, after cable patt, using needle 4, pick up 1 st in the thumb CO—39 sts.

Rnd 51: Using needle 1, pick up 3 more sts across the thumb CO, k18 across needles 1 and 2; needles 3 and 4: work cable patt rnd10, stopping before the last st of the patt (which would have been p1), using the last 2 sts on needle 4, p2tog—41 sts.

Rnd 52: Needles 1 and 2: k2, k2tog, k17; needles 3 and 4: work cable patt rnd 11—40 sts.

Rnd 53–77: Needles 1 and 2: k20; needles 3 and 4: work next right-hand cable patt rnd.

Rnd 78: K20 across needles 1 and 2; needles 3 and 4: work cable patt rnd 13.

Decreasing for Fingertip Area

Rnd 79: K4, k2tog, k3, k2tog, k3, k2tog, k4, p1, c2f, k2tog, p1, c2rp2, p2tog, p1, p2tog, p2, c2f, p1—34 sts.

Rnd 80: K17, p1, k2, p2, k2, p7, k2, p1.

Rnd 81: K3, k2tog, k2, k2tog, k3, k2tog, k3, p1, c2f, p2tog, k2, p1, p2tog, mb, p2tog, p1, c2f, p1—28 sts.

Rnd 82: K14, p1, k2, p1, ssk, p5, k2, p1—27 sts.

Rnd 83: [K2tog, k1] 4 times, k2tog, p1, ssk, p1, c1lp1, [p2tog] 2 times, ssk, p1—18 sts.

Rnd 84: K9, p1, k1, p2, k1, p2, k1, p1.

Rnd 85: K2tog, k1, k2tog, k2, [k2tog] 2 times, p2tog, k1, p2tog, ssk—11 sts.

Cut yarn, leaving an 8" [20.5 cm] tail. Thread tail through rem sts to close top of mitten.

Finishing

Weave in ends.

Note: Blocking the mittens will help to settle the cables and even out the slant of the zigzag cable, and it can also allow the mittens to fit larger hands (or smaller hands more loosely).

To block the mittens, wash them according to the yarn manufacturer's washing instructions and then press in a towel to remove excess water. Lay the mittens on a blocking board or folded towel and gently reshape them, tugging horizontally and vertically, as necessary, to increase their size. Resist the temptation to try on the mittens while they're still damp; doing so may stretch them out of shape.

Materials

- Rowan *Big Wool* (100% merino wool; 87 yd. [80 m] per 100 g ball), #43 Forest (color A), 1 ball, #37 Zing (color B), 1 ball, #16 Sugar Spun (color C), 1 ball, #08 Black (color D), 1 ball, and #24 Cassis (color E), 1 ball

Note: You can make two hats—one Child size and one Adult size—with one ball of each color.

- Or similar yarn that knits to specified gauge: super-bulky-weight wool or wool-blend yarn, about 87 yd. [80 m] each in 5 colors
- US 13 [9 mm] 16" [40 cm] circular needle
- US 13 [9 mm] double-pointed needles
- Stitch markers
- Tapestry needle

Gauge

10 sts and 14 rnds = 4" [10 cm] in St st using size 13 [9 mm] needles

Note: Gauge will probably vary between colorwork and solid color areas, and it may be necessary to use a larger or smaller needle size for some sections in order to maintain gauge.

RON'S ANIMAL CRACKERS HAT

Designer – Eileene Coscolluela ☽ *Pattern Rating – First Year*

Grab some magical animal crackers and get ready to roar! This fun and unusual hat, based on one worn by Ron Weasley in *Prisoner of Azkaban,* can be made in both child and adult sizes. With a single ball of each color, you'll have enough yarn to make one of each size, including the optional bow and braids. This project is great for a beginner wanting to learn colorwork; an advanced knitter can whip one up in an evening.

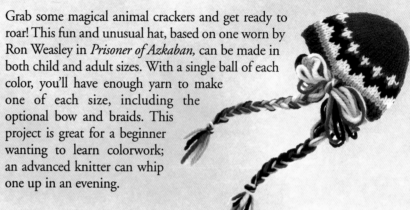

Instructions

With color A, CO 36 (48) sts, pm to note beg rnd, and join in a circle, being careful not to twist sts.

Brim

Work 3 rnds in single rib, as described in the stitch guide.

Hat Body

Work all 11 rnds of color chart on page 145.

Crown

As you decrease to shape the crown, change to dpns when too few sts rem to continue on circ needle.

Next rnd: Continuing with color A only, *k2, k2tog; rep from * to end of rnd—27 (36) sts.

Knit 4 (5) rnds.

Next rnd: *K2, k2tog; rep from * to last 3 (0) sts, k3 (0)—21 (27) sts.

Knit 2 (3) rnds.

Next rnd: *K1, k2tog; rep from * to end of rnd—14 (18) sts.

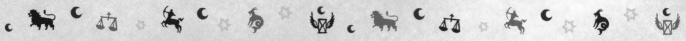

Knit 1 (2) rnds.

Next rnd: *K2tog; rep from * to end of rnd—7 (9) sts.

Cut yarn, leaving an 8" [20.5 cm] tail, and thread tail through rem sts to close top of hat.

Finishing

Weave in ends.

Block, if desired, according to yarn manufacturer's instructions.

Make Braids and Bow (Optional)

If you like, you can make the two braids and bow featured in the film version of the hat. The bow and braids are detachable but can be sewn into place, if desired.

Cut 2-yd. [2 m] strands of rem yarn—3 each of colors B, C, D, and E (12 strands total).

Loop 4 strands and thread them through the bottom knit st at center back ribbing. Loop next 4 strands through knit st above previous st. Loop last 4 strands through top knit st in same column.

Tie a bow centered in the middle of the lengths. Leave about 12" [30.5 cm] ends for braiding. For each of the two ends, divide into three 4-strand portions and braid, securing each braid with a knot.

Finished Size

Child (Adult)

Circumference: About 15 (20)" [38 (51) cm], slightly stretched

Length: 7 (8)" [18 (20.5) cm]

Samples shown: Sizes Child and Adult

Stitch Guide for This Project

Single Rib (1x1 Rib) Worked in Rounds

Rnd 1: *K1, p1; rep from * to end of rnd.

Rep rnd 1.

Stockinette Stitch (St st) Worked in Rounds

Knit all sts.

Key

☐	Knit each st in color as shown on chart
■	Forest - color A
■	Zing - color B
☐	Sugar Spun - color C
■	Black - color D
■	Cassis - color E
☐	Pattern repeat frame

11
10
9
8
7
6
5
4
3
2
1

Ron's Ragg Raglan

Designer – Jenn Jarvis ☾ *Pattern Rating – Ordinary Wizarding Level*

Mrs. Weasley's latest creation, we presume. Inspired by Ron's new initial sweater seen in *Goblet of Fire*, this funky update of the classic Weasley sweater sports raglan sleeves with button closures and a sewn-on initial. The super-soft marled Alpaca yarn makes the sweater a delight to wear while still giving it that Ragg look that says Weasley. The pattern is unisex, so the sweater should fit big kids, men, or women . . . just as well as any of Molly's sweaters ever do.

Body

Note: The sweater body is worked in the round up to the underarms. Then you put the body aside and work the sleeves in rows up to the armholes. Finally, all the pieces are brought together and the yoke is worked, partially in the round and then back and forth in rows once the sections for the button plackets are bound off.

CO 124 (136, 152, 168) sts onto circ needle. Pm to note beg rnd and join in a circle, being careful not to twist sts.

Work in double rib, as described in the stitch guide (see page 148), for 10 rnds.

Change to St st and work until body measures 15" [38 cm] from CO edge, ending last rnd 4 sts before marker at end of rnd.

Divide for front and back as follows:

Next rnd: *BO 8 sts, removing marker, and work until there are 54 (60, 68, 76) sts on right needle after BO section; rep from * to end of rnd—54 (60, 68, 76) sts each for front and back.

Cut yarn, leaving an 8" [20.5 cm] tail, and place sts on holders or scrap yarn for later.

Materials

- Misti *Alpaca Chunky* (100% baby alpaca, 108 yd. [99 m] per 100 g skein): #471 Black/Gray Moulinette, 8 (9, 11, 12) skeins
- Or similar yarn that knits to specified gauge: chunky-weight alpaca or wool yarn, about 780 (870, 980, 1,130) yd. [713 (796, 896, 1,033) m]
- US 9 [5.5 mm] 24" [60 cm] circular needle
- Stitch holders
- Stitch markers
- Tapestry needle
- ¼ yd. [23 cm] red velvet fabric
- Fusible interfacing (optional)
- 8 1" [2.5 cm] black buttons
- Gold and black thread
- Sewing needle

Gauge

15 sts and 20 rows = 4" [10 cm] in St st using size 9 [5.5 mm] needles

Finished Size

Child L (Adult S, Adult M, Adult L)

To fit chest: 30 (32/34, 36/38, 40/42)" [76 (81.5/86.5, 91.5/96.5, 101.5/106.5) cm]

Finished chest circumference: 33 (36¼, 40½, 44¾)" [84 (92, 103, 113.5) cm]

Length: 22¾ (24, 24¾, 25½)" [58 (61, 63, 65) cm]

Sample shown: Size Adult S

Stitch Guide for This Project

Double Rib (2x2) Worked in Rounds

Row 1: *K2, p2; rep from * to end.

Rep row 1.

Stockinette St (St st) Worked in Rounds

Knit all sts.

Double Rib (2x2) Worked in Rows Over a Multiple of 4 Sts Plus 2

Row 1: *K2, p2; rep from * to last 2 sts, k2.

Row 2: P2, *k2, p2; rep from * to end of row.

Rep rows 1 and 2.

Stockinette St Worked in Rows

Row 1 (RS): Knit.

Row 2 (WS): Purl.

Rep rows 1 and 2.

Double Rib (2x2) Worked in Rows Over a Multiple of 4 Sts

Row 1 (RS): K3, * p2, k2; rep from * to last st, k1.

Row 2 (WS): P3, * k2, p2; rep from * to last st, p1.

Rep rows 1 and 2.

Sleeves

CO 38 (38, 42, 42) sts. Work in double rib for 10 rows.

Work 2 rows in St st, beginning with a knit row.

> **Next row (inc row):** K1, m1, knit to last st, m1, k1—(40, 40, 44, 44) sts.

Work this inc row every 18th (11th, 14th, 10th) row 3 (5, 4, 6) times more—46 (50, 52, 56) sts.

Work even until sleeve measures 17 (17, 18, 18)" [43 (43, 45.5, 45.5) cm] from CO edge, ending with a WS row completed.

BO 4 sts beg next 2 rows—38 (42, 44, 48) sts.

After completing first sleeve, cut yarn, leaving an 8" [20.5 cm] tail, and place sts on a holder.

Make second sleeve the same. After completing second sleeve, leave sts on needle. Do not cut yarn.

Yoke

Slip sts for front, right sleeve, and back onto circ needle after second sleeve. With yarn still attached to sleeve, k38 (42, 44, 48) sts of left sleeve, pm, k54 (60, 68, 76) sts of front, pm, k38 (42, 44, 48) sts of right sleeve, pm, k54 (60, 68,76) sts of back, pm—184 (204, 224, 248) sts.

Join in a circle, being careful not to twist sts, and work 2 rnds in St st.

Decrease Yoke

Begin yoke decreases as follows:

Next rnd (dec rnd): *K1, k2tog, knit to 3 sts before marker, ssk, k1, slip marker; rep from * to end of rnd—176 (196, 216, 240) sts.

Work 3 rnds even in St st.

Note: At this point, you divide the yoke into two unequal sections (the front panel makes up one section and, together, the back and sleeves make up the second section).

Next rnd (dec rnd): K1, k2tog, knit to 3 sts before marker, ssk, k1, remove marker, k1, BO next 4 sts for left front raglan seam, k1, k2tog, knit to 9 sts before next marker, ssk, k2, BO next 4 sts for right front raglan seam, remove marker, k1, k2tog, knit to 3 sts before marker, ssk, k1, slip marker, k1, k2tog, knit to 3 sts before final marker, ssk, k1—40 (46, 54, 62) sts on front section; 120 (134, 146, 162) sts on back section.

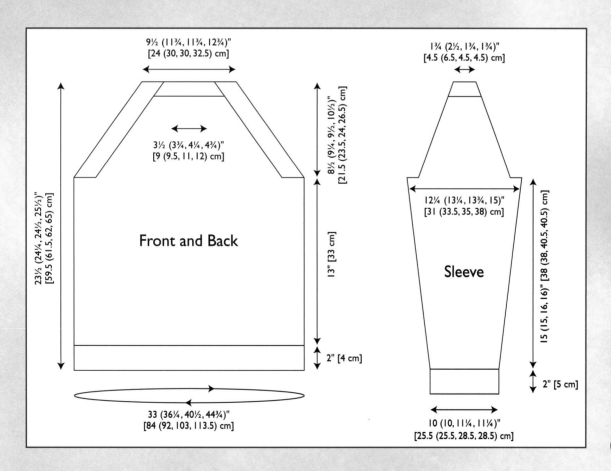

Front and Back

9½ (11¾, 11¾, 12¾)" [24 (30, 30, 32.5) cm]

3½ (3¾, 4¼, 4¾)" [9 (9.5, 11, 12) cm]

8½ (9¼, 9½, 10½)" [21.5 (23.5, 24, 26.5) cm]

23½ (24¼, 24½, 25½)" [59.5 (61.5, 62, 65) cm]

13" [33 cm]

2" [4 cm]

33 (36¼, 40½, 44¾)" [84 (92, 103, 113.5) cm]

Sleeve

1¾ (2½, 1¾, 1¾)" [4.5 (6.5, 4.5, 4.5) cm]

12¼ (13¼, 13¾, 15)" [31 (33.5, 35, 38) cm]

15 (15, 16, 16)" [38 (38, 40.5, 40.5) cm]

2" [5 cm]

10 (10, 11¼, 11¼)" [25.5 (25.5, 28.5, 28.5) cm]

Cut yarn, leaving an 8" [20.5 cm] tail. Sl sts from first sleeve onto right needle so entire back section is together.

Work Front and Back

Work remainder of piece back and forth in rows, working front section (front panel only) and back section (back and both sleeves) at the same time, as follows:

> **Next row (WS):** Attach yarn to back section, purl across, slipping markers; attach second ball of yarn to front section, purl across, turn.

Work 2 rows of each section even in St st.

> **Next row (RS):** Front: k2, k2tog, knit to last 4 sts, ssk, k2—38 (44, 52, 60) sts; back: k2, k2tog, knit to 3 sts before marker, ssk, k1, slip marker, k1, k2tog, knit to 3 sts before marker, ssk, k1, slip marker, k1, k2tog, knit to last 4 sts, ssk, k2; turn—114 (128, 140, 156) sts (2 sts decreased on front; 6 sts decreased on back)
>
> **Next row (WS):** Purl.

Rep last 2 rows 13 (14, 16, 18) times more, until 12 (16, 20, 24) sts rem for front and 36 (44, 44, 48) sts rem for back.

Work in double rib for 1" [2.5 cm]. BO all sts in patt.

Finishing

Graft bound-off underarm sts together (see page 160). Weave in ends.

Block, if desired, following yarn manufacturer's instructions.

Button Bands

With RS facing, pick up and k28 (32, 34, 36) sts along left raglan edge of back section. Work in St st for 4 rows. BO knitwise.

Sew top button 1" [2.5 cm] from top of band, sew bottom button 1" [2.5 cm] from bottom of band, and sew other buttons evenly between.

Rep for right back raglan edge.

Buttonhole Bands

With RS facing, pick up and k28 (32, 34, 36) sts along left front raglan edge. Purl 1 row.

> **Next row (RS—work buttonholes):** Knit across, working [yo, k2tog] buttonhole opposite each button on corresponding buttonband.

Work 2 more rows in St st. BO knitwise.

Sew bottom edge of buttonhole band to 4 BO sts on front raglan.

Rep for right front raglan edge.

Initial

Cut 7" [18 cm] square pieces of velvet and fusible interfacing. Iron together, following fusible interfacing instructions. Make template by drawing desired initial approx 6" [15 cm] square (or using a text editing program to create and print template). Cut out template, pin to fabric, and cut initial out of fabric. Outline initial with gold thread by hand or with sewing machine. Using photo for reference, whipstitch initial to front of sweater.